T0301802

An Analysis of

Søren Kierkegaard

Fear and Trembling

Brittany Pheiffer Noble

Published by Macat International Ltd
24:13 Coda Centre, 189 Munster Road, London SW6 6AW.

Distributed exclusively by Routledge
2 Park Square, Milton Park, Abingdon, Oxon OX14 4RN
711 Third Avenue, New York, NY 10017, USA

Routledge is an imprint of the Taylor & Francis Group, an informa business

www.macat.com
info@macat.com

Cataloguing in Publication Data
A catalogue record for this book is available from the British Library.
Library of Congress Cataloguing-in-Publication Data is available upon request.
Cover illustration: Etienne Gilfillan

ISBN 978-1-912303-04-5 (hardback)
ISBN 978-1-912127-74-0 (paperback)
ISBN 978-1-912281-92-3 (e-book)

Notice
The information in this book is designed to orientate readers of the work under analysis,
to elucidate and contextualise its key ideas and themes, and to aid in the development
of critical thinking skills. It is not meant to be used, nor should it be used, as a
substitute for original thinking or in place of original writing or research. References and
notes are provided for informational purposes and their presence does not constitute
endorsement of the information or opinions therein. This book is presented solely for
educational purposes. It is sold on the understanding that the publisher is not engaged
to provide any scholarly advice. The publisher has made every effort to ensure that
this book is accurate and up-to-date, but makes no warranties or representations with
regard to the completeness or reliability of the information it contains. The information
and the opinions provided herein are not guaranteed or warranted to produce particular
results and may not be suitable for students of every ability. The publisher shall not be
liable for any loss, damage or disruption arising from any errors or omissions, or from
the use of this book, including, but not limited to, special, incidental, consequential or
other damages caused, or alleged to have been caused, directly or indirectly, by the
information contained within.

CONTENTS

THE MACAT LIBRARY

The Macat Library is a series of unique academic explorations of seminal works in the humanities and social sciences – books and papers that have had a significant and widely recognised impact on their disciplines. It has been created to serve as much more than just a summary of what lies between the covers of a great book. It illuminates and explores the influences on, ideas of, and impact of that book. Our goal is to offer a learning resource that encourages critical thinking and fosters a better, deeper understanding of important ideas.

Each publication is divided into three Sections: Influences, Ideas, and Impact. Each Section has four Modules. These explore every important facet of the work, and the responses to it.

This Section-Module structure makes a Macat Library book easy to use, but it has another important feature. Because each Macat book is written to the same format, it is possible (and encouraged!) to cross-reference multiple Macat books along the same lines of inquiry or research. This allows the reader to open up interesting interdisciplinary pathways.

To further aid your reading, lists of glossary terms and people mentioned are included at the end of this book (these are indicated by an asterisk [*] throughout) – as well as a list of works cited.

Macat has worked with the University of Cambridge to identify the elements of critical thinking and understand the ways in which six different skills combine to enable effective thinking.
Three allow us to fully understand a problem; three more give us the tools to solve it. Together, these six skills make up the **PACIER** model of critical thinking. They are:

ANALYSIS – understanding how an argument is built
EVALUATION – exploring the strengths and weaknesses of an argument
INTERPRETATION – understanding issues of meaning

CREATIVE THINKING – coming up with new ideas and fresh connections
PROBLEM-SOLVING – producing strong solutions
REASONING – creating strong arguments

To find out more, visit **WWW.MACAT.COM.**

CRITICAL THINKING AND *FEAR AND TREMBLING*

Primary critical thinking skill: CREATIVE THINKING
Secondary critical thinking skill: REASONING

Danish philosopher Søren Kierkegaard's 1843 book *Fear and Trembling* shows precisely why he is regarded as one of the most significant and creative philosophers of the nineteenth century.

Creative thinkers can be many things, but one of their common attributes is an ability to redefine, reframe and reconsider problems from novel angles. In Kierkegaard's case, he chose to approach the problems of faith and ethics in a deliberately artful and non-systematic way. Writing under the pseudonym "John the Silent," he declared that he was "nothing of a philosopher," but an "amateur," wanting to write poetically and elegantly about the things that fascinated him. While *Fear and Trembling* is very much the work of a philosopher, Kierkegaard's protests showed his intent to take a different path, approaching his topic like no one else before him.

The book goes on to ask what the real nature of our personal relationship with God might be, and how faith might interact with ethics. What, Kierkegaard asks, can we make of God asking Abraham to sacrifice his only son, and of Abraham obeying? Arguing the unorthodox position that in following God's incomprehensible will Abraham had acted ethically, Kierkegaard set out the parameters of a moral argument that remains strikingly novel over a 150 years later.

ABOUT THE AUTHOR OF THE ORIGINAL WORK

Born in Copenhagen, Denmark in 1813, **Søren Kierkegaard** rarely left his hometown, travelling only to study briefly with philosophers in Germany. He never married, ending a brief engagement because he feared the commitment would interfere with his work. Inherited wealth allowed Kierkegaard to self-publish and he did so prolifically, mostly using a variety of pseudonyms. Yet, because he wrote in Danish, the philosopher remained relatively unknown outside of his home country until his works were translated into English and German in the early twentieth century. He died in 1855, aged just 42.

ABOUT THE AUTHOR OF THE ANALYSIS

Brittany Pheiffer Noble is a graduate student at Columbia University and holds a Masters degree from Yale University's Divinity School, where she studied religion and theology. Her research focuses on literary and aesthetic theory, alongside theology and history. She is the translator of Arab Orthodox Christians Under the Ottomans 1516–1831 (2016) and has taught at Sciences Po, Columbia and Dartmouth.

ABOUT MACAT

GREAT WORKS FOR CRITICAL THINKING

Macat is focused on making the ideas of the world's great thinkers accessible and comprehensible to everybody, everywhere, in ways that promote the development of enhanced critical thinking skills.

It works with leading academics from the world's top universities to produce new analyses that focus on the ideas and the impact of the most influential works ever written across a wide variety of academic disciplines. Each of the works that sit at the heart of its growing library is an enduring example of great thinking. But by setting them in context – and looking at the influences that shaped their authors, as well as the responses they provoked – Macat encourages readers to look at these classics and game-changers with fresh eyes. Readers learn to think, engage and challenge their ideas, rather than simply accepting them.

'Macat offers an amazing first-of-its-kind tool for interdisciplinary learning and research. Its focus on works that transformed their disciplines and its rigorous approach, drawing on the world's leading experts and educational institutions, opens up a world-class education to anyone.'

Andreas Schleicher
Director for Education and Skills, Organisation for Economic Co-operation and Development

'Macat is taking on some of the major challenges in university education … They have drawn together a strong team of active academics who are producing teaching materials that are novel in the breadth of their approach.'

Prof Lord Broers,
former Vice-Chancellor of the University of Cambridge

'The Macat vision is exceptionally exciting. It focuses upon new modes of learning which analyse and explain seminal texts which have profoundly influenced world thinking and so social and economic development. It promotes the kind of critical thinking which is essential for any society and economy. This is the learning of the future.'

Rt Hon Charles Clarke, former UK Secretary of State for Education

'The Macat analyses provide immediate access to the critical conversation surrounding the books that have shaped their respective discipline, which will make them an invaluable resource to all of those, students and teachers, working in the field.'

Professor William Tronzo, University of California at San Diego

WAYS IN TO THE TEXT

KEY POINTS

- Born in 1813, Søren Kierkegaard spent almost his entire life in his hometown of Copenhagen, Denmark. His family's wealth enabled him to self-publish all of his works, so he never had to worry about censorship.

- *Fear and Trembling* looks at the conflict between faith and established systems of ethics*—and the seeming absurdity of some of the demands God makes on the faithful.

- Kierkegaard counted himself as much an artist as a philosopher. He uses a mixture of story, poems, fables, and biblical passages to convey the ideas in Fear and Trembling.

Who Was Søren Kierkegaard?

Born in Copenhagen in 1813, Søren Kierkegaard rarely left his hometown, making an exception only to study briefly with philosophers in Germany. His family's wealth meant that he never had to worry about money; he could pursue a scholarly life and self-publish his works—escaping both editorial interference and censorship. A commercial publisher with an eye on profit would most likely have restricted his output. Kierkegaard wrote prolifically, often under a range of pseudonyms,* or pen names. In fact, in 1843, the year he published *Fear and Trembling*, he also released four other books.

In his 30s, Kierkegaard fell in love with a young woman named Regine Olsen.* After a long courtship, he asked her to marry him, and she accepted, but Kierkegaard broke off the engagement—partly because he felt his melancholy* personality made him poorly suited to marriage, and partly because he worried that the commitment of having a wife (and perhaps one day a family) would interfere with his writing. He viewed writing as his true calling. In part, *Fear and Trembling* represents Kierkegaard's attempt to make sense of this episode, and find a higher purpose in the sacrifice of his relationship.

Because Kierkegaard wrote in Danish, his native tongue, he remained virtually unknown outside Scandinavia during his lifetime. That began to change in the early twentieth century, when his books were translated into German and English. Today, while his works may not be seen as part of what would be considered core philosophical texts, his ideas remain influential in ongoing debates about religion, ethics, and the role of the individual in society.

What Does *Fear and Trembling* Say?

Does God ask us to do unethical things? That's the core question of *Fear and Trembling*, and Kierkegaard examines it principally by recounting the biblical story in which God commands Abraham* to sacrifice his only son, Isaac.

Other philosophers before Kierkegaard had analyzed this same story: Immanuel Kant* in the eighteenth century decided that God's command to Abraham was so unethical that the story rendered the entire Old Testament* suspect as a source of ethical guidance. Writing in the early nineteenth century, G. W. F. Hegel* did not consider Abraham's actions exemplary because they were the result of a problematic relationship with God. His analysis examined the relationship between Abraham and God, and Judaism* as a religion and culture. Kierkegaard reacted against both of these pillars of philosophical thought, arguing instead for an ethics based on each individual's relationship to God. No one but God could understand Abraham's actions, in Kierkegaard's reading, and since Abraham acted according to God's will, he had indeed acted ethically.

Fear and Trembling also introduces the "knight of faith,"* a concept Kierkegaard invented to embody the idea of someone whose faith in God survives through trials and hardships. For Kierkegaard, faith has two mandates. To become a "knight of faith" you have to turn your back on your personal desires (as Abraham did in being willing to sacrifice his son, the great love of his life, and as Kierkegaard did in breaking off his engagement), and maintain hope. The hope that God will somehow restore what was lost counteracts the overwhelming despair of losing it.

Each person who wants to be a "knight of faith" will face those two issues in his (for Kierkegaard it was always "his") own way. But in order to do so, at some point he must take a personal "leap of faith" and trust in God's purpose, as Abraham did.

Kierkegaard knew his interpretation of the Abraham story would shock his readers. He wanted to shake them up, to encourage them to reject their complacency. He believed the Church of Denmark supported and encouraged this complacency. He also felt that when the leaders of a country—and the vast majority of the population— all follow the same religious guidance, then it could only create conformity. In Kierkegaard's view, God wants each of us to choose to follow our *own* moral and ethical path—as Abraham did—even if it means we risk being misunderstood by those around us.

The novelty of Kierkegaard's argument is matched by his unique literary style. He wrote *Fear and Trembling* under the pseudonym Johannes de Silentio*—John the Silent. We should not assume that de Silentio's ideas match Kierkegaard's. In fact, the philosopher often used created characters like de Silentio to set up an argument. And on more than one occasion, he had a pseudonymous* author criticize or respond to the works of another of his pseudonymous authors.

This complexity has provided plenty of material for analysis. Scholars have always examined Kierkegaard's ideas from a religious or philosophical perspective. But, most recently, scholars of literature have begun to explore the rich textures of Kierkegaard's writing style and the way he shaped his ideas through the interplay among his stable of pseudonymous authors.

Why Does *Fear and Trembling* Matter?

Once Kierkegaard's works were translated into more widely spoken languages than Danish in the early twentieth century, they quickly became part of discussions of philosophy and religion. More recently they have been discussed in terms of literary criticism.

His ideas have moved rebels and revolutionaries from Dietrich Bonhoeffer*— executed by the Nazis* for plotting to kill Hitler* during World War II—to more peaceful practitioners of civil disobedience like Indian independence leader Mohandas K. Gandhi* and American civil rights champion the Reverend Martin Luther King, Jr.*

A prolific author, Kierkegaard wrote about many aspects of religion and philosophy. But perhaps his greatest contributions remain his writings on dread, anxiety, irony, love, and care. He also made telling distinctions in the aesthetic, ethical, and religious approaches to life. In *Fear and Trembling*, he focused primarily on how ethics and religion cross over—or diverge.

One of Kierkegaard's main aims in writing *Fear and Trembling* was to criticize the way his contemporaries blindly followed the teachings of the state Church. While there is still some interest in this today, the aspect of the book most often discussed now is one to which Kierkegaard's contemporaries paid little attention: his recognition that Christian* life, as God asks us to live it, can be fundamentally absurd. Following God's commands produces paradoxes for us, just as it did for Abraham, a highly ethical man who obeyed God's will while disobeying the absolute laws of ethics.

Fear and Trembling is essential reading for anyone wanting to learn more about how Kierkegaard's personal emotional challenges informed his philosophy. It's also key for readers who want to improve their own personal ethical and moral codes. As long as anxiety and hope remain universal human emotions, Kierkegaard's analysis of Abraham's actions in the face of God's command will be important to readers. As long as authorities—whether governments or religions—insist on (or even encourage) blind obedience to a fixed set of norms, Kierkegaard's insistence that it is an individual's responsibility to develop his or her own codes of faith and ethics will remain fresh and relevant. While Kierkegaard clearly writes from a Christian perspective, his thoughts have intrigued thinkers of all religious types, and even atheists.

Kierkegaard said that *Fear and Trembling* would establish a lasting reputation for him—the book was "enough for an imperishable name as an author."[1] While it took much longer than he could have predicted for this to happen, he was nonetheless correct about his work's enduring impact.

NOTES

1   Howard and Edna Hong, introduction to *Fear and Trembling/Repetition* by Søren Kierkegaard (Princeton: Princeton University Press, 1983), xxxiv.

SECTION 1
INFLUENCES

MODULE 1
THE AUTHOR AND THE HISTORICAL CONTEXT

KEY POINTS

- Søren Kierkegaard's *Fear and Trembling* challenges the philosophical systems of its time. Through biblical interpretation, allegories* and philosophical meditations, the work proposes an alternative vision of an individual's ethical* responsibility.

- Two aspects of Kierkegaard's life shape this work: his religious devotion and a failed love affair. The former drives his search for a meaningful life of faith, and the latter drives his quest to resist despair in the face of disappointment.

- Kierkegaard wrote *Fear and Trembling* in 1843 after he had visited Germany and studied German philosophy.

Why Read This Text?

Søren Kierkegaard's 1843 work *Fear and Trembling* is a unique project in the tradition of European philosophy. It responds to and challenges previous ideas, building on his lifelong project of exploring the different—and sometimes opposing—realms of the ethical and the religious.

Kierkegaard does this in *Fear and Trembling* by examining the biblical story of the Binding of Isaac.* In the Book of Genesis,* God orders Abraham* to kill his only child, Isaac, as a sacrifice. Abraham obeys, preparing his son for the ritual. Only at the very last moment, as Abraham raises a knife to his bound son, does an angel of God prevent the slaughter. Kierkegaard uses this story to investigate the dilemma of modern faith, with Abraham as a model of what faith looks like.

15

** ❝ An entry on Abraham [by Kierkegaard] from 1843 has been turned around by some interpreters of *Fear and Trembling* and used as a justification for a primarily biographical approach to the work: 'He who has explained this riddle has explained my life.' ❞**

Howard and Edna Hong, Introduction to *Fear and Trembling*

In Kierkegaard's view, real faith should be difficult and require trust in God. But in modern times, religious life had become comfortable, easy and undemanding. The politics of the day and rivalries between institutional figures within the Church of Denmark drove Kierkegaard's condemnation of institutional Christianity.* He hoped this book would be read by everyone, from philosophers and the clerical Establishment to the popular masses.

Author's Life

Born in 1813 into a well-to-do family, Søren Kierkegaard spent almost his entire life in his hometown of Copenhagen, Denmark. He left only for short trips to Germany. His great personal wealth allowed him to lead a scholarly life. Like most Danes, Kierkegaard's family was Protestant* and they were members of the official Church of Denmark. His father was a deeply religious man whose severe self-criticism and anxieties about divine judgment—how God would view his life—profoundly affected Kierkegaard.

Kierkegaard published *Fear and Trembling* in 1843, as soon as he had finished writing it. He had already established himself as a major figure in Copenhagen's literary world, having written a number of books and contributed frequently to local journals. Originally published in Kierkegaard's native tongue of Danish, *Fear and Trembling* did not become accessible to a wide audience until scholars translated it into German and English in the twentieth century.

Because he was wealthy enough to self-publish his works, Kierkegaard maintained full creative control over his writing. Although his work was never officially censored, it still attracted criticism. Over the course of Kierkegaard's career, local journals or newspapers critiqued or satirized him for a variety of faults or eccentricities. By the 1850s (seven years after *Fear and Trembling*), deep anxieties about the way the public responded shaped Kierkegaard's writings. He lived the last few years of his life in virtual isolation. In addition to criticizing the passive and easy religious life of the day, *Fear and Trembling* revisits a deeply personal loss in Kierkegaard's life. In 1841, he broke off his engagement with Regine Olsen,* the woman he had loved for years. She loved him too. But Kierkegaard ended their relationship, fearing his moodiness made him unsuited to marriage and that marriage might constrain him from pursuing his true calling, philosophy.

Later readers have called *Fear and Trembling* "existentialist."* Existentialism is a term applied to a type of philosophy or literature that values the individual's wholly unique experience of life as a thinking, feeling subject. The book has been considered as existentialist for two reasons: the personal way in which it grapples with the loss of a loved one and the narrator's anxiety about how each person's unique position in life shapes how they must live.

Author's Background

Kierkegaard was strongly influenced by the religious environment of his time. In Denmark, the state Church was (and still is) Lutheran, a mainstream denomination of Protestantism that celebrates two Christian rituals, baptism and Communion, and follows the teachings of the religious reformer Martin Luther.* Danish Protestantism shaped Kiekegaard's personal, social, and theological outlook. Yet at this time various factions—favoring either reform or conservatism—competed for dominance in the Church. These social and political skirmishes made Kierkegaard concerned about issues of religion, ecclesiology* (the theological study of the Church) and Church authority for the rest of his life.

At the time Kierkegaard wrote *Fear and Trembling* there were two major issues concerning philosophers: history and ethics.* These discussions stemmed in general from two notions. First there was G. W. F. Hegel's* earlier nineteenth-century philosophy of the teleological* progression of history. This was the idea that history progresses *toward* something and that it is neither meaningless nor regressive. Second there was Immanuel Kant's* late eighteenth-century belief in absolute morals. Kant said that, ethically speaking, we must always do what is right and that we cannot alter right and wrong according to specific situations. Kierkegaard studied and reacted to both philosophies.

Unlike Hegel, Kierkegaard often insisted that modern times were no better than the past. He regretted the lack of sincere faith, piety, or religious passion in his day and laid the blame for this on the political-ecclesiastical* status quo of Denmark. Everyone attended the state's Church, and Kierkegaard thought this allowed people not to have to think about what it meant *to them* to be a Christian or take any individual responsibility for their faith.

Unlike Kant, Kierkegaard rejects the notion of absolute ethics or morality. In *Fear and Trembling* this takes shape in his retelling of the story of Abraham, who came close to sacrificing his only son for God.

Kierkegaard wrote *Fear and Trembling* under the pseudonym* Johannes de Silentio*—John the Silent. He rarely published under his own name, but he did not use pseudonyms* as mere disguises. His pseudonyms are characters in and of themselves. Readers should not confuse them with Kierkegaard as a person.[1] In this analysis, we refer to Kierkegaard as the historical figure responsible for *Fear and Trembling*, but within the context of the ideas proposed in the text, the author is de Silentio.

NOTES

1   For a useful introduction to the de Silentio pseudonym, see Michael Weston's *Kierkegaard and Modern Continental Philosophy: An Introduction* (London: Routledge, 1994), 11–16.

MODULE 2
ACADEMIC CONTEXT

KEY POINTS

- Kierkegaard wrote during a period in which the philosophy known as German Idealism* was very influential. Philosophers in this tradition created metaphysical systems of thought to explain the interior and exterior life of humans.

- Immanuel Kant's* earlier philosophy critiqued human reason, proposed that God is unknowable, and argued for an absolute system of ethics.* German Idealist philosophers often developed these subjects.

- Kierkegaard responds to the major German philosophers of his time, namely Hegel,* Kant, and Schelling,* and in particular challenges their systems of ethics with his ideas in *Fear and Trembling*.

The Work in its Context

When Søren Kierkegaard wrote *Fear and Trembling*, German philosophers dominated the philosophical landscape. Immanuel Kant had made enormous contributions to philosophy, especially in his 1781 work *Critique of Pure Reason*.[1] Generations later, philosophers were still responding to his ideas. Of particular importance in the post-Kantian period are the Germans G. W. F. Hegel, Johann Gottlieb Fichte,* and Friedrich Schelling. Kierkegaard studied under Schelling in Berlin. These post-Kantian philosophers belong to a school of philosophy known as German Idealism.

Kant claimed there was a huge difference between what could be perceived and what lay beyond human perception. He maintained that realities existed beyond human experience and dubbed them

❝ ... 'Truth,' Hegel says, is seen as the end of thought. It is revealed where thought attains its telos, which is something to be determined by *thinking itself.* The truth is not something external to thought to which it may correspond and which would allow the possibility of the skeptical question, but is rather the immanent goal thought is itself directed towards... **❞**

Michael Weston, *Kierkegaard and Modern Continental Philosophy*

noumena, * or "things-in-themselves." Kant believed these *noumena* are not the invention of human perception or reason.

The later German Idealists disagreed. After Kant, many thinkers would critique the idea of things having an essence completely divorced from human reason and perception. They would also criticize the notion that some things were entirely beyond human perception, and so could not be examined by philosophy.

Another important distinction philosophers made during this time was between the "inner" and the "outer" realms of human experience. For Hegel, the inner life (that is, the life of the mind and contemplation) was greater than the outer life, which consisted of physical things. The German Idealists, including a subgroup known as Transcendental Idealists, concerned themselves mostly with what one can understand based on the inner life. They argued that we can base knowledge on subjective experiences and that we can experience God through contemplation.

Overview of the Field

One of Immanuel Kant's main concerns was ethics. For Kant, killing an innocent person is unethical, so you cannot use religion or God as an excuse to break the rules of ethics. Since Abraham stands ready to kill his own child because he wants to obey God, Kant sees the biblical story Kierkegaard would later treat in *Fear and Trembling* as highly unethical.

Two other German philosophers who were particularly important to Kierkegaard are Fichte and Schelling. While both were concerned with human consciousness, Fichte in particular attempted to create a philosophy of the self that did not rely on Kantian categories. Fichte's thought is dubbed Transcendental Idealism to distinguish it as a subcategory within the larger tradition of German Idealism. Schelling focused on religion and mysticism. In particular, he explored notions of human freedom and how freedom could be understood by positive and negative theologies. Negative theology attempts to describe something by talking about what it is not, rather than what is. For example, a negative theological statement about God would be: "God is not limited by time." Positive theology, on the other hand, attempts to describe God with positive categories— in terms of what he is like. Kierkegaard attended Schelling's lectures in Berlin during one of his few trips abroad.

Academic Influences

In *Fear and Trembling*, Kierkegaard responds to a number of issues that were being discussed in his day. He also raises entirely new questions. Like much European philosophy at the time, Danish philosophy concerned itself with the teachings of Hegel, Schelling, and Kant. By the time Kierkegaard wrote, their ideas were widely spread and well accepted. Kierkegaard concerns himself specifically with their ideas about ethics and whether the religious teachings of Christianity* fit within current philosophical systems.

The ancient philosophers also influenced Kierkegaard, particularly the method of philosophical discussion and thinking found in Socrates* and Plato.* Fascinated by the question of whether it is the philosopher or the poet who can best tell the truth (that is, do humans understand things better through reason or through art?), Kierkegaard blends philosophical reasoning with poetic writing in all his works. Translators and Kierkegaard scholars Howard and Edna Hong* emphasize that Socrates was a prototype for Kierkegaard. Specifically, they point out that the Socratic method of teaching—in which the teacher and the student have an ongoing conversation and the experience of interaction is fundamental to learning—was very important to Kierkegaard.[2]

Two Danish professors who particularly influenced Kierkegaard, meanwhile, were Jacob Mynster* and Johan Heiberg.* Both were well-known figures in mid-nineteenth-century Copenhagen. Mynster had a great deal of institutional support from both the university and the Church. In time, he would be made a bishop. Heiberg was a public figure and frequent author of satires. Like Mynster, he also had very clear—and largely conservative—views on aesthetics* and formal art. Heiberg shared Kierkegaard's concern with the spiritual state of the middle-class public. They both believed the public focused more on material well-being than on any genuine spirituality or genuine religious feeling.

NOTES

1   Immanuel Kant, *Critique of Pure Reason*, trans. Werner Pluhar (Indianapolis: Hackett Publishing Co., 1996).

2   Howard and Edna Hong, introduction to *Fear and Trembling/Repetition* by Søren Kierkegaard (Princeton: Princeton University Press, 1983), xii.

23

THE PROBLEM

KEY POINTS

- Kierkegaard approaches the contemporary problems of ethics* and their universality by analyzing the biblical story of Abraham* and Isaac.

- Previous philosophers read the story differently. Kant* saw ethics as absolute and unvarying. Hegel,* less interested in ethics, focused on the psychology of Abraham that informs his relationship with God.

- Kierkegaard rejects Kant's ethics by arguing that a religious duty to God suspends an ethical obligation and criticizes Hegel for not engaging with the ethical and moral dimensions of Abraham's behavior.

Core Question

Søren Kierkegaard's *Fear and Trembling* poses the core question of whether we can act unethically while following our faith. Its other key questions—Does God ask us to do unethical things? What are the limits of ethics? What is the psychological consequence of acting on faith?—emerge from this core question. Kierkegaard makes the novel proposal that the individual's responsibility is based on his or her unique relationship with God.

Kierkegaard uses the Old Testament* story of the Binding of Isaac* and the way it explores the meaning of sacrifice to question the existential* part of faith. Kierkegaard uses the word "existential" to refer to how the *individual*—in this case Abraham—experiences this demand and sacrifice personally and internally, *not* as a member of a religious group. He finds a paradox

❝ At the first and most apparent level of meaning, *Fear and Trembling* is a stinging critique of both the popular and cultured Christianity of his day and a reminder of the primitive challenge of Christian faith. ❞

Ronald Green, *The Cambridge Companion to Kierkegaard*

in the story of Abraham sacrificing Isaac: Murder goes against the rules of ethics, but disobeying God goes against the rules of faith. And the individual must grapple with this paradox alone.

In his role as the writer Johannes de Silentio,* Kierkegaard considers whether it would have been ethical for Abraham to kill Isaac because God commanded it. As one scholar summarizes the problem of the work, the Abraham story "… conveys a new emphasis on faith as a way of life. This emphasis is meant to replace the centuries-old understanding of faith as merely an acceptance of dogmatic truths."[1]

Fear and Trembling asks if Abraham was right to be *willing* to kill his son. Bringing the biblical story into the contemporary world, de Silentio wonders what would happen if a man heard a sermon about Abraham and then decided to kill his own son. How can we make sense of this story? In this line of inquiry, de Silentio questions the entire ethical framework that makes it possible to commit murder as an act of religious obedience.

The Participants

Scholars see *Fear and Trembling* as a self-conscious critique of two of the major thinkers in the European philosophical landscape: Immanuel Kant and G. W. F. Hegel. Hegel had floated the notion of collective histories—the histories of societies, nations, and epochs.* Kant had proposed universal ethics. But de Silentio challenges elements of both philosophers' readings of the Binding of Isaac.

Hegel's belief is that man is obliged to act based on an objective reasoning, which in turn means he must be bound by objective laws. A subjective viewpoint cannot override questions of right and wrong.

For Hegel, righteous Jews* follow the law of God unswervingly because their entire relationship with God is organized around laws. They are unable to break free of this oppressive legal relationship. If they could interact with God as an individual—determining their own personal decisions and behavior based not on laws, but on objective rights and wrongs—they would become more self-conscious as human actors, which is an important virtue for Hegel.

Hegel understands Abraham as a man alienated by the Jewish law that isolates him from God and the natural world. Abraham's dilemma—obey moral law or obey God—is grounded in his obedience to Jewish law. He has a slave-like relationship to God.

While Hegel focuses on social or collective events, de Silentio concerns himself with personal history, personal choices, and personal action. As de Silentio sees it, Abraham, in his willingness to sacrifice Isaac, acts out of his personal will and his relationship with God, not out of an obligation to his family, clan, or people. De Silentio criticizes Hegel for not condemning Abraham. He insists that in his treatment of the Binding of Isaac, Hegel fails to maintain his own ethical system. Hegel allows for Abraham's behavior because he sees it as an example of slavish obedience, ignoring the fact that this slavish obedience involves the murder of an innocent child.

Kant primarily argued that Abraham should not have agreed to break the moral law in the first place, since there was no way for him to know that he was really hearing God's voice.[2] But de Silentio rejects the universal ethical standard of Kant's philosophy. For de Silentio, Abraham stands ready to break the ethical standard, and this is not even in pursuit of a higher ethical good. For him, it is crucial that Abraham's actions display a "teleological* suspension of the ethical."[3] Teleological means something destined or ultimately meant for a certain goal or aim. The "teleological suspension of the ethical" is the notion that one can, in a certain instance, act contrary to common ethical standards for the sake of something greater. The laws of ethics must condemn Abraham's behavior, but as de Silentio sees it, because Abraham acted out of faith and sacrifice, we may see his actions as exemplary, not atrocious.

The Contemporary Debate

In *Fear and Trembling*, Kierkegaard responds to thinkers from previous generations who could never reply to him. Immanuel Kant died more than 30 years before Kierkegaard wrote the book, and G. W. F. Hegel had been gone for a decade. Also, because he published *Fear and Trembling* in his native Danish rather than German, the immediate successors of Hegel's and Kant's philosophy—primarily working in Germany—were not able to read and react to Kierkegaard's ideas. One Hegelian* in Denmark, Bishop Jacob Mynster,* called *Fear and Trembling* "remarkable."[4] But this response never sparked any sustained debate over the text.

Although largely ignored when it was published in 1843, *Fear and Trembling* became accessible to a much wider community of philosophers and theologians once German- and English-speaking scholars translated it in the early years of the twentieth century. So while there was little or no contemporary debate about *Fear and Trembling* during Kierkegaard's life, 60 years or so after its publication the work took a central place in discussions of philosophy and ethics. Later scholars in Scandinavia and beyond would find much more of value in *Fear and Trembling* than any of Kierkegaard's fellow scholars did during his lifetime.

NOTES

1   Ronald M. Green, "'Developing' *Fear and Trembling*," in *The Cambridge Companion to Kierkegaard*, ed. Alastair Hannay and Gordon D. Marino (Cambridge: Cambridge University Press, 1998), 259.

2   Immanuel Kant, *The Conflict of the Faculties*, trans. Mary J. Gregor (Lincoln: University of Nebraska Press, 1992), 115.

3   Søren Kierkegaard, *Fear and Trembling/Repetition*, trans. Howard and Edna Hong (Princeton: Princeton University Press, 1983), 54.

4   Howard and Edna Hong, introduction to *Fear and Trembling/Repetition* by Søren Kierkegaard (Princeton: Princeton University Press, 1983), xxxvi.

MODULE 4
THE AUTHOR'S CONTRIBUTION

KEY POINTS

- De Silentio* meditates on how we cannot understand Abraham's* willingness to kill his own son by applying external morals. We can only understand it by examining the inner relationship of Abraham to God.

- He develops a philosophical defense of Abraham and also considers the emotional and psychological dimensions of Abraham's experience.

- *Fear and Trembling* approaches the distinction between the inner and outer life in a new way and argues for the superiority of religious life over ethical life.*

Author's Aims

Themes of sacrifice and renunciation* resonate in a highly personal way throughout Søren Kierkegaard's work, and especially in *Fear and Trembling*. In this book, Kierkegaard addresses anxiety, resignation,* faith, sacrifice, and the disparity between ethics* in the outer world and the inner life of faith and obedience. Imagining his readers to be middle- or upper-middle-class Protestants* attending the state Church, Kierkegaard proposes that each of us, in our own unique relationship with God, can potentially live in faithful communion with God. This challenges previously articulated systems of thought (moral, ethical, religious, or philosophical) that set forth universal standards by which everyone must abide.

Kierkegaard also had strong personal concerns about an individual's relationships with others. He particularly struggled with institutions that make claims on one's duty and commitment, such as marriage.

❝ It takes a purely human courage to renounce the whole temporal realm in order to gain eternity, but this I do gain and in all eternity can never renounce—it is a self-contradiction. But it takes a paradoxical and humble courage to grasp the whole temporal realm now by virtue of the absurd, and this is the courage of faith. By faith Abraham did not renounce Isaac, but by faith Abraham received Isaac."❞

Søren Kierkegaard, *Fear and Trembling*

Two years before publishing *Fear and Trembling*, he suddenly broke off his engagement to the woman he loved, Regine Olsen.*[1] Two factors drove this event: First, Kierkegaard feared he was not suited to marriage. Second, he worried that marriage would negatively impact his ability to pursue his spiritual calling, his work. But he struggled to believe that in ending his engagement he had acted in the best interest of both parties, not just himself. Scholars accept that in writing *Fear and Trembling* Kierkegaard aimed, at least partly, to find a philosophical and religious justification for his actions. This painful episode would haunt many of his later writings, but when he wrote *Fear and Trembling* the wound was still fresh.

Approach

Kierkegaard does not just challenge philosophical ideas in *Fear and Trembling*. He also provides a model of how Christians* may live a life of sacrifice. In his view, such a life is marked by resignation, faith, and a confrontation with the absurd.

According to *Fear and Trembling*, the ideal Christian life begins with resignation, or the giving up of one's desires. After resignation, Christians must have faith—which means retaining hope that what was lost will be restored.

Kierkegaard does not think that this renunciation must always be externally apparent. It might be an inner renunciation that no one can see, turning one's will toward God. He links this invisible renunciation to isolation. Those around you cannot understand what you are going through or comprehend the logic of your obedience to God. This was certainly true of Isaac and of Abraham's wife Sarah in the Old Testament* story of the Binding of Isaac.*

De Silentio* points out that we cannot just emulate Abraham's actions. The lesson God wants us to take from the story is too counterintuitive and challenging to accept easily. The actions God asks Abraham to take are absurd. De Silentio writes, "He [Abraham] acts by virtue of the absurd, for it is precisely the absurd that he as the single individual is higher than the universal. This paradox cannot be mediated … He gets Isaac back again by virtue of the absurd."[2] Yet even though we may not be able to comprehend God's will or the absurd situation, Abraham's actions remain valid.

With its terrifying demand (to kill one's child) and absurd logic (it is right to kill the child), the Binding of Isaac shows Christians how Christian life diverges from the simple rules of regular life. It also shows how a Christian must be willing to do things he doesn't understand. This paradox of obedience and the confrontation with the absurd would make Kierkegaard's moral lesson of Abraham troubling and problematic for later readers.

Contribution in Context

Written in an intellectual environment dominated by German Idealism,* *Fear and Trembling* largely rejects the widely accepted ethics of G. W. F. Hegel* and Immanuel Kant.* Instead, Kierkegaard proposes something altogether new: an ethical code based on each individual's unique relationship with God—even if that relationship makes incomprehensible demands on the individual.

In the previous century, Kant had argued that Abraham was unethical in being willing to murder his son, Isaac, at God's request in the Book of Genesis,* Chapter 22 in the Old Testament. For Kant, this made reading the Old Testament for moral guidance problematic.[3] Under normal circumstances, killing one's own child—or, indeed, any innocent person—obviously violates standard ethical codes. To Kant, Abraham's unethical, immoral behavior renders the entire Old Testament untrustworthy as a source of ethical guidance.

Modern American scholar Ronald Green* contends that in *Fear and Trembling*, Kierkegaard directly addresses Kant's treatment of Abraham. In fact, Green considers *Fear and Trembling* a direct assault on any "rationalist philosophy (including Hegel's) that underestimates the seriousness of sin and the radical measures needed to overcome it."[4] Not all later scholars read *Fear and Trembling*'s treatment of ethics as wholly incompatible with Kant's. But most agree that Kierkegaard lays down a challenge to Kant here.

NOTES

1 Kierkegaard broke off his engagement with Regine Olsen in 1841, after nearly a year, ostensibly because he felt he could not reconcile his melancholy nature and his desire to pursue a writing career with the commitment of marriage.

2 Søren Kierkegaard, *Fear and Trembling/Repetition*, trans. Howard and Edna Hong (Princeton: Princeton University Press, 1983), 56.

3 Ronald M. Green, "'Developing' *Fear and Trembling*," in *The Cambridge Companion to Kierkegaard*, ed. Alastair Hannay and Gordon D. Marino (Cambridge: Cambridge University Press, 1998), 270.

4 Green, "'Developing' *Fear and Trembling*," 270.

SECTION 2
IDEAS

MAIN IDEAS

KEY POINTS

- *Fear and Trembling* examines what the life of faith really is; the difference between ethical life* and religious life and the spiritual and psychological experiences of dread and anxiety.

- De Silentio* uses the story of the Binding of Isaac* to show that the life of faith is based on a unique relationship to God rather than on generic ethical norms.

- He retells the Binding of Isaac in four ways and puts forward three major questions arising from the story. He then brings up more recent stories for additional perspectives on the problems.

Key Themes

Søren Kierkegaard's *Fear and Trembling* asks: What happens when religious responsibility comes into conflict with ethics?* Can we ever justify breaking the rules of ethics on religious grounds? And if we do break the rules of ethics to follow something we must do from a religious perspective, then what are the consequences? The key themes arising from these questions are ethics, faith, obedience, resignation,* and isolation.

Abraham's* willingness to sacrifice his son forms the central theme of *Fear and Trembling*. De Silentio, the pseudonymous* author of the book, begins by imagining four different scenes in which Abraham leads his son, Isaac, up the mountain to be sacrificed.

Then de Silentio reflects on what it meant for Abraham to be willing to obey God's command to commit murder. He considers

f The story of Abraham contains just such a teleological suspension of the ethical ... If one looks more closely, I doubt very much that anyone in the whole wide world will find one single analogy ... [Abraham's] life not only is the most paradoxical that can be thought but is also so paradoxical that it simply cannot be thought. He acts by virtue of the absurd, for it is precisely the absurd that he as the single individual is higher than the universal. ™

Søren Kierkegaard, *Fear and Trembling*

the effect this act would have had. If Abraham had carried out his actions, his family would have been forever marked by violence and tragedy. In particular, de Silentio considers anxiety, dread, and resignation as part of Abraham's experience.

Fear and Trembling looks to Abraham as a model of righteousness. How could a man of faith have been willing to kill his own son? At the crux of the dilemma of faith, obedience, and morality, de Silentio finds the notion that each man has his own relationship to God and a personal "leap" he must make into faith. The title Kierkegaard chose for his work explicitly links the Abraham narrative with the Christian* message of salvation in the Bible's New Testament where Saint Paul* writes: " ... continue to work out your salvation with fear and trembling."[1]

Exploring the Ideas

In *Fear and Trembling*, de Silentio identifies two steps Abraham had to take as he journeyed up Mount Moriah with his son. First, he had to renounce his desires: while his son was his greatest love, his obedience to God had to take precedence. Second, Abraham had to embrace hope. In doing this he became a "knight of faith,*"[2] someone who still hopes—even in the face of resignation—that God will restore what has been lost or sacrificed. The author proposes this hope as the necessary antidote to the overwhelming despair produced by the renunciation* of desire.

After discussing the story of Abraham, de Silentio poses three *problemata** (Greek for "problems") to address an ethical question that would presumably be solved by the system Hegel* outlined in his *Elements of the Philosophy of Right*.[3]. In that work, published more than two decades earlier, Hegel argues that man must act according to objective reasoning and be subject to objective laws: a person's subjective perception or position should not interfere with questions of right and wrong. In demonstrating how the story of Abraham contradicts Hegel's answer, de Silentio challenges readers to reimagine their own ethical and religious duties.

The first problem—and the study's most pressing question—raises the possibility that Abraham acted within the bounds of Hegel's universal ethical system, having necessarily broken, or suspended, the ethical in order to obey God. To be sure, being willing to murder suspends regular ethics. But by calling this suspension "teleological,"* de Silentio insists that the suspension has a higher purpose. With a real goal and aim, it is not random or meaningless, but a *specific* instance where human actions overcome the ethical.

Both the second and third problems investigate the notion of horror and isolation as a key part of the Binding of Isaac. De Silentio writes, the "true knight of faith is always [in] absolute isolation … he is the single individual, simple and solely the single individual without any connections and complications."[4]

Before returning to the paradox of the knight of faith, the third problem considers other stories of love, sacrifice, and tragedy. Abraham's silence isolates him. As he cannot tell either his wife or his son what he is going through, he remains silent in his resignation to God.

Language and Expression

Kierkegaard used a vast collection of pseudonyms* for his works, and certain constructed figures "authored" multiple works. Pseudonyms served as more than a way of obscuring Kierkegaard's identity. As a literary device, they allowed him to look at his philosophical claims from many perspectives. Not everything a pseudonymous author says represents Kierkegaard's personal stance. Sometimes the invented authors float ideas with which Kierkegaard disagrees—and which he will later critique under a different pen name.

Kierkegaard believed the most important religious truths "cannot be communicated directly," but that creativity in the writing could help the reader understand them.[5] He never explicitly tells his reader what to believe. Instead he offers a variety of positions, illustrating the various shortcomings of each. He doesn't just speak in the language of philosophy, either. He enriches his investigation by quoting stories, poems, biblical passages, and fables. Since he uses a variety of literary styles and devices in his text, recent scholars have begun to study Kierkegaard's work purely for its literary merit.

Fear and Trembling serves as a bridge of sorts, linking serious philosophical problems with meditations on the personal life and on how Christians must live in the face of anxiety, suffering, loss, and hope. After *Fear and Trembling*, Kierkegaard's works such as 1843's *Upbuilding Discourses*[6] became more explicitly about religious devotion. All of Kierkegaard's later works contain traces of his investigations into anxiety, faith, and the religious or ethical life, but he first addressed these issues in *Fear and Trembling*.[7]

NOTES

1   Saint Paul, "Letter to the Philippians," 2:12.

2   The "knight of faith" is a figure described by Kierkegaard as someone who appears to be normal—nothing particular in appearance, wealth, piety, or social position—but who is special because he (or she) takes joy in life, is not attached to "worldly" things, and lives "by virtue of the absurd." For a much lengthier portrait, see Kierkegaard's description in *Fear and Trembling*, 38–41.

3   Georg Wilhelm Fredrich Hegel, *Elements of the Philosophy of Right*, trans. H. B. Nisbet (Cambridge: Cambridge University Press, 1991).

4   Søren Kierkegaard, *Fear and Trembling/Repetition*, trans. Howard and Edna Hong (Princeton: Princeton University Press, 1983), 79.

5   Ronald M. Green, "'Developing' *Fear and Trembling*," in *The Cambridge Companion to Kierkegaard*, ed. Alastair Hannay and Gordon D. Marino (Cambridge: Cambridge University Press, 1998), 257.

6   Søren Kierkegaard, *Eighteen Upbuilding Discourses*, trans. Howard Hong and Edna Hong (Princeton: Princeton University Press, 1990).

7   Joakim Garff, *Søren Kierkegaard: A Biography*, trans. Bruce H. Kirmmse (Princeton: Princeton University Press, 2007), 252–65.

MODULE 6
SECONDARY IDEAS

KEY POINTS

- De Silentio* proposes the figure of the "knight of faith"*
  as a model for Christian* living. The life of faith contains a
  paradox and this paradox of faith becomes the next point
  of inquiry.

- The book's secondary themes highlight how complex the
  life of faith is, and how no simple (or even complicated)
  philosophical system can explain away the contradictions
  inherent in a faithful life.

- The "knight of faith" should be a model for the reader for
  how to live and persevere in the face of despair, disbelief,
  or disappointment.

Other Ideas

An important concept Søren Kierkegaard (as Johannes de Silentio)
introduces in *Fear and Trembling* is that of the "knight of faith"—those
who rely on their faith in God in the face of hardship, disappointment,
and their own inability to renounce their personal desires. As American
scholar Roland Green* explains, "Johannes [de Silentio] lets us know
that the capacity for such knighthood is not confined to the older
heroes and saints of faith but remains available to every human being.
He imagines a knight of faith residing in the Copenhagen of his day."[1]

Fear and Trembling explores the concept of the "knight of faith"
by putting the figure of Abraham* in relief against the philosophy of
Hegel.* Its reversal of Hegel's hierarchy concerning a person's outer
and inner life remains one of the most powerful contributions *Fear
and Trembling* has made to philosophy.

❝ Let us consider in somewhat more detail the distress and anxiety in the paradox of faith. The tragic hero relinquishes himself in order to express the universal; the knight of faith relinquishes the universal in order to become the single individual. As said previously, everything depends on one's position. Anyone who believes that it is fairly easy to be the single individual can always be sure that he is not a knight of faith, for fly-by-nights and itinerant geniuses are not men of faith. ❞

Søren Kierkegaard, *Fear and Trembling*

Hegel put forward the idea that the outer life (*das Äussere*), which other people can observe, reflects the essence of the person. He further argues that this outer life is more important than a person's private, inner life (*das Innere*).[2] De Silentio argues that Abraham's story inverts Hegel's notion, writing that: "faith is the paradox that interiority is higher than exteriority."[3] De Silentio's discussion of the "knight of faith" expands on the challenges of living in this paradox.

Exploring the Ideas

Fear and Trembling makes the argument that an absolute duty to God can give rise to a paradox, something that seems self-contradictory or self-negating. One might wonder how a God who gives us a moral code and supposedly expresses himself as love can demand that we break the moral code and kill that which we love. No rational thought can help people make sense of such a paradox. The only course left is to take a leap of faith. Abraham confronted this paradox directly and his behavior remained incomprehensible to anyone other than himself.

Fear and Trembling also investigates the notion of anxiety. De Silentio writes: "The ethical expression for what Abraham did is that he meant to murder Isaac; the religious expression is that he meant to sacrifice Isaac—but precisely in this contradiction is the anxiety that can make a person sleepless, and yet without this anxiety Abraham is not who he is."[4]

Anxiety—self-doubt, worry, uncertainty as to how things will work out—remains a fundamental part of the Christian life. Because faith means acting in the face of uncertainty, the true knight of faith must suffer anxiety while trusting that he will be delivered from anxiety by God.

While the ethical life* has absolute rules, de Silentio explains: "It is different in the world of the spirit. Here an eternal divine order prevails. Here it does not rain on both the just and the unjust; here the sun does not shine on both good and evil. Here it holds true that only the one who works gets bread, that only the one who was in anxiety finds rest, that only the one who descends into the lower world rescues the beloved, that only the one who draws the knife gets Isaac."[5]

Johannes de Silentio offers this as some comfort to the reader who seeks to become a knight of faith: he sees the isolation and silence that arise from obedience not as signs of failure, but as an inherent part of the paradox of faith.

Overlooked

While *Fear and Trembling* and Kierkegaard's other works have been widely analyzed, scholars have only recently begun to analyze Kierkegaard's actual writing style. He communicates his ideas creatively and indirectly—hiding behind a pseudonym,* telling stories, and even making seemingly contradictory statements.

As American Kierkegaard scholars Howard and Edna Hong* wrote in 1983, Kierkegaard believes "an author's private experience can legitimately be used in his writing only in transmuted form, that is, as the universally human, not as personal disclosure … Kierkegaard expressly employed indirect communication in works such as *Fear and Trembling* and *Repetition** in order to take himself as author out of the picture and to leave the reader alone with the ideas."[6]

Another little-studied facet of Kierkegaard's work is the quality of his writing as literary prose—as art, rather than just a medium for conveying philosophical claims. This scholarly omission stems largely from the fact that scholars who are not fluent in Danish must rely on translations. In the last few decades, revised translations have allowed for greater analysis of the text. But no one has yet employed philology*—a combination of linguistics, literary criticism, and history—to analyze Kierkegaard's work.

American Kierkegaard scholar Ronald Green* argues that scholars have overlooked the discussion of sin in *Fear and Trembling*.[7] For Green, de Silentio's story of the merman*—a fantastical blend of human and fish—in the final *problemata** not only offers a parallel to Abraham, but also directly engages with the notion of sin. In the fairy tale, the merman seduces and falls in love with a human woman named Agnes. He then faces a dilemma. He had intended to trick Agnes into following him into the sea, but realizing that she is innocent and genuinely loves him, he wonders whether he should confess, maintain the deceit, or resort to magic. Ultimately, he returns her to her home, telling her only that he wanted to show her the sea and not mentioning his seduction plan.

In Green's view, the merman's story shows how sin, like faith, suspends the ethical and brings one into direct relationship with God. Like Abraham, the merman planned to kill one he loved; like Abraham, he does not follow through on that plan. (And, we must note, like Kierkegaard, the merman voluntarily surrenders his beloved.) Scholar Steven Mulhall* has also written on the role of sin in *Fear and Trembling* and other Kierkegaard works. However, most secular (non-religious) philosophers and theorists tend to shy away from the word "sin." So we have much left to learn about Kierkegaard's idea of sin as an inversion of faith that happens outside the realm of ethics.*

NOTES

1   Ronald M. Green, "'Developing' *Fear and Trembling*," in *The Cambridge Companion to Kierkegaard*, ed. Alastair Hannay and Gordon D. Marino (Cambridge: Cambridge University Press, 1998), 261.

2   Michael Inwood, ed., "Inner and Outer, Internal and External," in *A Hegel Dictionary* (Blackwell Publishing, Blackwell Reference Online), accessed April 13, 2015, www.blackwellreference.com/subscriber/tocnode. html?id=g9780631175339_chunk_g978063117533913_ss1-9 .

3   Søren Kierkegaard, *Fear and Trembling/Repetition*, trans. Howard and Edna Hong (Princeton: Princeton University Press, 1983), 69.

4   Kierkegaard, *Fear and Trembling*, 30.

5   Kierkegaard, *Fear and Trembling*, 27.

6   Howard and Edna Hong, introduction to *Fear and Trembling/Repetition* by Søren Kierkegaard (Princeton: Princeton University Press, 1983), x.

7   Green, "'Developing' *Fear and Trembling*," 272–3.

MODULE 7
ACHIEVEMENT

KEY POINTS

- Kierkegaard regarded *Fear and Trembling* as a worthy investigation into the problems captivating him.

- The book was written during a very fruitful time in his life. Because he could self-publish, he did not have to arrange funding or worry about outside editorial interference with his text.

- *Fear and Trembling* was not well received and would only become popular after Kierkegaard's death in 1855, a dozen years after it was published.

Assessing the Argument

In *Fear and Trembling,* Søren Kierkegaard aims to shock the reader into a new understanding of the horrifying nature of the demands God made of Abraham.* Kierkegaard wants his readers to reject interpretations that separate Abraham's dilemma from the kinds of decisions they might make in their own lives.[1]

Fear and Trembling insists that Abraham should not remain simply a historical figure. Kierkegaard wants his timeless would-be sacrifice to resonate with the modern reader. Nor does the writer see Abraham as a tragic figure like a Greek hero. In Greek tragedies, the hero sacrifices him- or herself for the community or a clear higher good—such as by dying in battle, dying for the beliefs of the community, or sacrificing oneself to save another's life.

Because Abraham's community had nothing to gain from Isaac's death, the sacrifice he stood ready to make surpassed even those of Greek tragedy.

❝ Once I am dead, *Fear and Trembling* alone will be enough for an imperishable name as an author. Then it will be read, translated into foreign languages as well. **❞**

Søren Kierkegaard, Notes to *Fear and Trembling*

Kierkegaard was highly satisfied with his work in *Fear and Trembling*. And how could he not be, since he controlled the entire editing and publication process? But he was by no means finished with the themes *Fear and Trembling* explores. He revisited its ideas in *Repetition** (1843), *The Concept of Anxiety* (1844), *Philosophical Fragments* (1844), and *Concluding Unscientific Postscript to the Philosophical Fragments* (1846).[2]

Achievement in Context

Initial responses to Kierkegaard's work, including *Fear and Trembling*, were not positive. The first commentary to be published on him was actually a "seal of disapproval" of his thinking.[3] But scholars now recognize *Fear and Trembling* as a complex work that remains relevant to contemporary society.

Translations—which began to appear in the early years of the twentieth century—have been key to this reversal of opinion, as most scholars cannot read the work in the original Danish. American clergyman Walter Lowrie's* translations introduced Kierkegaard to the English-speaking world. But Lowrie's translations focused far more on the religious aspect of the text than on its literary quality. As another scholar wrote: "The fact that the original translators were theologians or philosophers of religion has had a decisive effect upon the way that Kierkegaard has been received in the United States and indeed throughout the English-speaking world. There was from the first a remarkably impoverished awareness of Kierkegaard as a writer, as a stylist and as a rhetorician."[4] The more nuanced later translations have in some part remedied this shortcoming.

Another reason *Fear and Trembling* has not had a greater presence in the philosophical debate is that major thinkers of the past century, such as German philosopher Martin Heidegger,* failed to acknowledge Kierkegaard as an influence.[5] On the other hand, such diverse twentieth-century thinkers as German philosophers Carl Schmitt* and Karl Jaspers,* and French philosophers Jean-Paul Sartre* and Jacques Derrida,* have explicitly acknowledged his influence.

Limitations

In some ways, *Fear and Trembling* acknowledges that a gulf exists between text and reader. Indeed, the Abraham we encounter in the Binding of Isaac* remains unknowable—even to those who would like to imitate his faith. Still, the concerns raised in *Fear and Trembling* may be more easily accessible in some cultures than others.

Modern Western readers, accustomed to a clear separation between Church and state, may find it difficult to understand some of Kierkegaard's critique of the state Church of Denmark. Still, anyone in a society where one religion predominates can imagine the potential costs of enshrining that religion in government policy. We may read *Fear and Trembling* as a critique of any society or institution that demands loyalty at the cost of personal integrity or faith.

We might also see it as a critique of any community that elevates popular norms above personal convictions. By the mid-twentieth century, even atheist readers began to apply Kierkegaard's teachings to their own increasingly secular societies. They turned to him as an alternative to any system advocating universal ethics.*

Critics of traditional European philosophical debates—articulated by Friedrich Nietzsche* in the nineteenth century and Martin Heidegger in the twentieth—see an ally in Kierkegaard, who prioritized the individual over both the masses and abstract concepts.[6] After World Wars I and II,* Kierkegaard's readers saw his critique of modernity as particularly farsighted.

Some, such as the French philosopher and writer Jean-Paul Sartre, hesitated to use Kierkegaard's works because of Kierkegaard's associations with Christianity.*[7] Yet thinkers have increasingly recognized the connection between existentialism* and Kierkegaard—something Sartre explored in his *Being and Nothingness*:[8] "The central idea, however, of personal authenticity, of the avoidance of *mauvaise foi*,* indeed the entire scope of the existentialist notion of a free and responsible human life in a world of 'bourgeois' hypocrisy and mediocrity, is in fact Kierkegaardian, however little it may be acknowledged."[9]

Others, such as Sartre's fellow countryman and contemporary Jacques Derrida, found it possible to accept Kierkegaard's ideas without feeling compromised by his inherently Christian position.

NOTES

1   Alastair Hannay, "Faith and Tragic Heroism," in *Kierkegaard: A Biography* (Cambridge: Cambridge University Press, 2003), 180–206.

2   Howard and Edna Hong, introduction to *Fear and Trembling/Repetition* by Søren Kierkegaard (Princeton: Princeton University Press, 1983), xxxi. See also Søren Kierkegaard, *The Concept of Anxiety*, trans. Reidar Thomte (Princeton: Princeton University Press, 1981); Kierkegaard, *Philosophical Fragments*, trans. Howard and Edna Hong (Princeton: Princeton University Press, 1985); Kierkegaard, *Concluding Unscientific Postscript to Philosophical Fragments*, trans. Howard and Edna Hong (Princeton: Princeton University Press, 1992).

3   Ronald M. Green, "'Developing' *Fear and Trembling*," in *The Cambridge Companion to Kierkegaard*, ed. Alastair Hannay and Gordon D. Marino (Cambridge: Cambridge University Press, 1998), 270.

4   Roger Poole, "The Unknown Kierkegaard: Twentieth-Century Receptions," in *The Cambridge Companion to Kierkegaard*, ed. Alastair Hannay and Gordon D. Marino (Cambridge: Cambridge University Press, 1998) 59.

5   See an extended discussion of this in Poole, "The Unknown Kierkegaard."

6   Michael Weston, "Kierkegaard, Heidegger and the Problem of Existence," in *Kierkegaard and Modern Continental Philosophy: An Introduction* (London: Routledge, 1994), 33–57.

7   Poole, "The Unknown Kierkegaard," 54.

8   See Jean-Paul Sartre, *Being and Nothingness*, trans. Hazel Barnes (New York: Washington Square Press, 1992).

9   Poole, "The Unknown Kierkegaard," 54.

PLACE IN THE AUTHOR'S WORK

KEY POINTS

- Kierkegaard produced a range of philosophical and devotional* works concerned with aesthetics,* morality, Christianity,* faith, psychology, and social critique.

- *Fear and Trembling* deals with themes common to Kierkegaard's body of work, such as religion, ethics,* and the individual.

- Considered a seminal text for those studying Kierkegaard, *Fear and Trembling* remains one of his more popular works.

Positioning

Even though it is one of his early works, 1843's *Fear and Trembling* represents Søren Kierkegaard's mature thinking. It also provides a complex consideration of issues that featured in a work he published earlier that same year, called *Either/Or.*[1]

Because his family's wealth gave Kierkegaard the means to self-publish, no one limited his prolific output and no editor or censor tinkered with his ideas. By the time he released *Fear and Trembling*, he had become a major figure in the literary world of Copenhagen. A prolific author, he had already published a number of other books and he contributed frequently to local journals. During his life, however, his fame remained limited to Scandinavia. While most other major philosophers of his time wrote in German, Kierkegaard wrote in Danish, his native tongue. The first translations of his work would not arrive for some six decades: into German in 1909 and then into English in 1919.[2]

❝ Later [Kierkegaard] wrote, 'I am a poet. But long before I became a poet I was intended for the life of religious individuality. And the event whereby I became a poet was an ethical break or a teleological suspension of the ethical. And both of these things make me want to be something more than 'the poet' ...' ❞

Howard and Edna Hong, Introduction to *Fear and Trembling*

The dilemmas Kierkegaard presents in *Fear and Trembling* echo within the wider context of his large philosophical output. *Fear and Trembling* anticipates both Kierkegaard's long-term investigation into anxiety and his often-discussed division between the ethical and the religious.

For many reasons—including its tone, its philosophical concerns, and its assortment of literary examples—scholars consider *Fear and Trembling* thoroughly characteristic of Kierkegaard's work. It is also one of his most deeply personal books. *Fear and Trembling* marks a groundbreaking move in European philosophy toward what twentieth-century philosophers would call existentialism.*

Integration

Kierkegaard's large body of work allows us to see how his philosophical argument progressed. It also allows us to listen in on a dialogue between Kierkegaard and his pseudonymous* authors. As Kierkegaard's biographers point out, "the author of *Fear and Trembling*, Johannes de Silentio,* appears in the journals and papers as the possible author of a collection of aphorisms, some of which later appeared in *The Moment* but without Johannes de Silentio's name attached."[3] This dialogue between texts allows the careful reader to examine how Kierkegaard sometimes distances himself from the ideas proposed by his authorial personas.

Kierkegaard often investigated multiple angles of a problem or question through stories, legends, and poetry—as he did in *Fear and Trembling*. In revisiting these themes in other works, he would merely adopt different techniques. For example, *Either/Or*—a long, two-part study written just before *Fear and Trembling*—also investigates the separation of the religious and the ethical life. But it takes a broader scope than *Fear and Trembling*, examining the aesthetic life as well. Kierkegaard also touched on major themes expressed in *Fear and Trembling* in his books *Repetition** (1843), *The Concept of Anxiety* (1844), *Philosophical Fragments* (1844), *Stages on Life's Way* (1845), *Concluding Unscientific Postscript to the Philosophical Fragments* (1846), and *The Sickness unto Death* (1849).[4]

Significance

Since the early twentieth century—when they were first translated into languages other than Danish—*Fear and Trembling* and Kierkegaard's other works have played an important role in philosophical, religious, and literary discussions.

Kierkegaard's reflections on the importance of each unique person and the individual's power to make decisions and act resonate throughout history in many ways. The early investigations by nineteenth-century German philosopher Friedrich Nietzsche* and mid-twentieth-century existentialism draw from his work.[5] Kierkegaard's influence remains vivid and compelling even into the twenty-first century. Poststructuralists*—theorists who reject the idea that human culture can be clearly understood by analyzing linguistic or social structures—and contemporary theological scholars also cite Kierkegaard as an inspiration.

Arguably, Kierkegaard's thoughts on dread, anxiety, irony, love, and care and the distinction between the aesthetic, ethical, and religious lives remain his greatest contributions to religious and philosophical thinking. *Fear and Trembling* deals particularly with dread and the ethical and religious life. German philosopher Martin Heidegger* and French existentialist philosophers Jean-Paul Sartre* and Albert Camus* owe a particular debt to Kierkegaard's multifaceted exploration of the psychological, religious, ethical, and philosophical dimensions of the experience of dread.[6] Kierkegaard's critique of complacent Christianity in *Fear and Trembling* and other works would resonate strongly with post-World War II* thinkers in Europe. They read it as a foreshadowing of the conditions that produced the war.

Like much of Kierkegaard's work, *Fear and Trembling* has had a major influence on the discipline of philosophy. Scholars also see it as laying the groundwork for important twentieth-century developments such as the concept of civil disobedience,* by teaching the importance of the individual over and against the values of worldly institutions or communities. *Fear and Trembling* lays the theological groundwork for the Christian to understand that he or she is responsible to God, not to society and not to the government.

NOTES

1   Joakim Garff, *Søren Kierkegaard: A Biography*, trans. Bruce H. Kirmmse (Princeton: Princeton University Press, 2007), 252. See Søren Kierkegaard, *Either/Or*, trans. Howard and Edna Hong (Princeton: Princeton University Press, 1987).

2   Jon Bartley Stewart, ed., *Kierkegaard's Influence on Theology: German Protestant Theology* (Farnham: Ashgate Publishing, 2012), 290.

3   Howard and Edna Hong, introduction to *Fear and Trembling/Repetition* by Søren Kierkegaard (Princeton: Princeton University Press, 1983), xxxiv. See Kierkegaard, *The Moment and Late Writings*, trans. Howard and Edna Hong (Princeton: Princeton University Press, 2009).

4   See Søren Kierkegaard, *Fear and Trembling/Repetition*, trans. Howard and Edna Hong (Princeton: Princeton University Press, 1983); Kierkegaard, *The Concept of Anxiety*, trans. Reidar Thomte (Princeton: Princeton University Press, 1981); Kierkegaard, *Philosophical Fragments*, trans. Howard and Edna Hong (Princeton: Princeton University Press, 1985); Kierkegaard,

Stages on Life's Way, trans. Howard and Edna Hong (Princeton: Princeton University Press, 1988); Kierkegaard, *Concluding Unscientific Postscript to Philosophical Fragments,* trans. Howard Hong and Edna Hong (Princeton: Princeton University Press, 1992); Kierkegaard, *The Sickness unto Death*, trans. Howard and Edna Hong (Princeton: Princeton University Press, 1983).

5   Nietzsche did not read Kierkegaard's words himself, since they weren't available yet in German. However, he read secondary literature in German that discussed Kierkegaard's ideas.

6   Michael Weston, "Kierkegaard, Heidegger and the Problem of Existence," in *Kierkegaard and Modern Continental Philosophy: An Introduction* (London: Routledge, 1994), 33–57. For more on Sartre and Kierkegaard, see William McBride's "Sartre's Debts to Kierkegaard: A Partial Reckoning," in *Kierkegaard in Post/Modernity*, ed. Martin Matustik and Merold Westphal (Bloomington and Indianapolis: Indiana University Press 1995), 18–42.

SECTION 3
IMPACT

THE FIRST RESPONSES

KEY POINTS

- *Fear and Trembling* generated very little response when it was first published, and early reviewers did not recognize Kierkegaard as the writer behind the pseudonym* of Johannes de Silentio.*

- No important responses to *Fear and Trembling* would emerge until many years after Kierkegaard's death.

- Translation played a crucial role in bringing Kierkegaard's writing to a wider audience. His works did not receive serious consideration outside of Denmark until they were translated into German, French, and English.

Criticism

Søren Kierkegaard published *Fear and Trembling* using the pseudonym Johannes de Silentio, so early readers did not realize he was, in fact, the author of the work. Kierkegaard often used pseudonyms. He attributed his book *Repetition*,*[1] a work he published at the same time as *Fear and Trembling*, to a writer called Constantine Constantius.* Early reviewers correctly guessed that the author of *Fear and Trembling* was the same person who had written *Either/Or*,[2] which had been published under the pseudonym Johannes Climacus.* However, it appears that critics directed very little attention at Kierkegaard personally in the early reviews.

Fear and Trembling didn't sell well. In the first four years after it was published in 1843, the book sold just 321 copies. In 1847, Kierkegaard remaindered* 204 copies—putting them up for sale at a greatly reduced price.[3] In general, though, the reviews were not bad, and most critics

> **"**One lingering myth about Kierkegaard is that he is an irrationalist in some sense that denies the value of clear and honest thinking. Kierkegaard did deny the ability of reasoned thought to arrive at universal and objective truth on matters of value, but today that is considered quite rational. **"**
>
> Alastair Hannay and Gordon D. Marino, *The Cambridge Companion to Kierkegaard*

praised Kierkegaard (or de Silentio) for his beautiful prose and style.

The first review—written by Johan F. Hagen, a student of the philosopher Hans Lassen Martensen*—praised both *Fear and Trembling* and *Either/Or* for their "dialectical talent and … penchant for paradox."[4] However, the reviewer questioned Kierkegaard's insistence on the importance of transcendence* and the absurd, arguing that faith could still fall within a rational system.

Jakob P. Mynster,* an influential Danish bishop and contemporary of Kierkegaard, did not review *Fear and Trembling* as such, but praised it highly in an article. Other minor reviews appeared anonymously, but they tended toward summary rather than analysis.

The initial criticism of *Fear and Trembling* had almost no impact on its later reception. None of Kierkegaard's early Danish detractors would ever approach the fame or influence of his later German and French supporters. This meant the less than glowing reviews *Fear and Trembling* received in the 1840s had no effect on the work's later reception.

Responses

Kierkegaard often wrote responses to his critics but he never mailed or published them, so we know of no sustained debate arising after the publication of *Fear and Trembling*.

Kierkegaard did, however, come very close to mailing a rebuttal to the Icelandic theologian Magnús Eiríksson,* who wrote under the name Theophilius Nicolaus. In his 1850 critique of *Fear and Trembling*, Nicolaus specifically took issue with Kierkegaard's treatment of "the absurd."[5] However, in the end, Kierkegaard did not send his views, so the public never heard any counterarguments to the criticism. Kierkegaard grew increasingly private and spent his last years in self-imposed isolation before his death in 1855. Scholars have no evidence of any significant public conversation or debate about *Fear and Trembling* after Nicolaus's 1850 critique.

Howard and Edna Hong,* American translators of Kierkegaard, contend that "The unpublished responses to the few reviews of both [*Fear and Trembling* and *Repetition*] did not occupy much of Kierkegaard's time and attention. He was already immersed in the writing of *Three Upbuilding Discourses*."[6] This was a remarkably prolific period of his life. In the years that followed, Kierkegaard threw himself into writing and publishing original works, often returning to ideas he had first raised in *Fear and Trembling* or *Either/Or*.

Conflict and Consensus

Kierkegaard never edited or amended *Fear and Trembling*—not to appease or enlighten his critics and not for his own purposes. Rather than rewrite it, he merely revisited its themes in later works. This does not imply that Kierkegaard disagreed with anything in *Fear and Trembling*. Instead, he preferred to hone important ideas and truths by constantly reworking them from a variety of perspectives.

Interestingly, later readers of *Fear and Trembling* would embrace the aspect of the book that most annoyed Kierkegaard's contemporaries: his recognition of the absurd and the paradoxical in the Christian* life. Kierkegaard's persistent drive to reject the comprehensive or universal systems laid out by preceding philosophers like G. W. F. Hegel* or Immanuel Kant* set an example for later scholars working in existentialist,* deconstructionist,* and postmodern* models.

Kierkegaard's contemporary critics apparently did not respond to the thinly veiled criticisms of the clergy and institutional Church in *Fear and Trembling*. They largely overlooked the social dimension of the work. But this dimension would become central in twentieth-century readings. Even as European and American societies become increasingly secular (non–religious), Kierkegaard's image of the "knight of faith"* operating outside of the established Church endures.

NOTES

1   Søren Kierkegaard, *Fear and Trembling/Repetition*, trans. Howard and Edna Hong (Princeton: Princeton University Press, 1983).

2   Søren Kierkegaard, *Either/Or*, trans. Howard and Edna Hong (Princeton: Princeton University Press, 1987).

3   Howard and Edna Hong, introduction to *Fear and Trembling/Repetition* by Søren Kierkegaard (Princeton: Princeton University Press, 1983), xxxv.

4   Howard and Edna Hong, introduction, xxxv.

5   Howard and Edna Hong, introduction, xxxviii.

6   Howard and Edna Hong, introduction, xxxviii. See *Three Upbuilding Discourses* in Søren Kierkegaard, *Eighteen Upbuilding Discourses*, trans. Howard and Edna Hong (Princeton: Princeton University Press, 1990).

MODULE 10
THE EVOLVING DEBATE

KEY POINTS

- Kierkegaard insisted on the individual being most important. In contemporary times, that has become part of a larger theological conversation about the individual's responsibility in the face of religious or cultural pressures.

- Kierkegaard's work has spawned no clearly defined schools of thought, but his influence is widely felt today in the disciplines of philosophy and theology.

- *Fear and Trembling* challenged the systematic framework of nineteenth-century philosophy and inspired twentieth-century philosophies that value the individual, the absurd, paradox, and the psychological complexity of modern life.

Uses and Problems

Søren Kierkegaard returned to concepts he raised in *Fear and Trembling* in many other works—and he would even reference his alter-ego de Silentio's* work. But he would never again do a focused study of the story of Abraham.*

Translators and American Kierkegaard scholars Howard and Edna Hong* point out: "The themes of *Fear and Trembling* that reappear in the journals and papers with specific reference to the work are: Abraham, 'the leap, becoming open and making manifest, the hero of faith,' the absurd, the single individual, and the poet and hero. An entry on Abraham from 1843 has been turned around by some interpreters of *Fear and Trembling* and used as a justification for a primarily biographical approach to the work: 'He who has explained this riddle has explained my life.'"[1]

❝ This chameleon-like quality of the Kierkegaard reception can be, and has been, blamed on Kierkegaard himself, on his resort to pseudonymity and on the variety of his themes and writing styles; one gets the impression that behind the writings no one in particular is at home ... Postmodern perspectivism provides yet another illustration of the versatile tenacity of Kierkegaard's appeal ... ❞

Alastair Hannay and Gordon D. Marino, *The Cambridge Companion to Kierkegaard*

Some see *Fear and Trembling* as a crucial work for anyone wishing to learn more about Kierkegaard's personal world. Studies linking Kierkegaard's relationship with Regine Olsen* to his philosophical inquiries focus on *Fear and Trembling*. In terms of philosophical content, scholars often consider *Either/Or*—published the same year—as an almost direct expansion of the ideas in *Fear and Trembling*, particularly the division between the ethical and the religious.[2] The discussion in *Either/Or* centers on the distinction between the aesthetic life* and the ethical life.* Kierkegaard finds that both fall short of the religious life.

Kierkegaard deeply influenced some of the greatest theological, political, and philosophical thinkers of the twentieth century. Two French philosophers, Emmanuel Lévinas* and Jacques Derrida,* quarreled over the meaning of *Fear and Trembling*. Derrida, who grappled explicitly with Kierkegaard's thoughts in his work *The Gift of Death*,[3] saw *Fear and Trembling* as an invitation to argue for ethics* as being a category of its own, independent of religion. Lévinas pushed against the project of creating an all-encompassing ethics.[4]

Schools of Thought

With its consideration of the ethical, theological, and psychological dimensions of faith, *Fear and Trembling* remains relevant both in academic studies and in practical study for the life of faith. The book's critique of Denmark's institutional Church, which Kierkegaard saw as "Christendom"* rather than as living Christianity,* resonates with different camps of modern thinkers who aim to critique Christianity. It also echoes in secular society at large, particularly in the West.

Kierkegaard's work has not spawned any specific school of thought. Scholars of Kierkegaard tend to be interested in existentialism* and nineteenth- and twentieth-century European philosophy (a large, diverse category known as continental philosophy).*

Current debate on *Fear and Trembling* has no central geographic, ideological, or religious focus. It crosses the line between academia and popular debate, as well as the borders between the United States, Europe, and beyond. Unlike the reaction to Kierkegaard that early twentieth-century theologians of Germany, France, and Switzerland arguably shared, today's debate takes place among a loose network of interested scholars, readers, public intellectuals, and literary theorists.

In Current Scholarship

In the past half-century, many of *Fear and Trembling*'s readers have overlooked the text's disagreements with Hegel* and Kant.* Those arguments were undoubtedly important to Kierkegaard, because the works of those two German philosophers had most influence on his own efforts. However, modern readers view *Fear and Trembling* as a more independent and radical text that can speak to contemporary philosophical questions. For instance, today's readers examine the themes of love, trust, and sin in the work. These new areas of investigation reveal the extent to which contemporary Kierkegaard scholarship is fueled by theological as much as philosophical or literary concerns.

Kierkegaard's writings have also had a serious impact on literature, notably on the work of Henrik Ibsen,* the Norwegian playwright best known for *A Doll's House*, written in 1879 and still frequently performed today. The way Ibsen brought Kierkegaard into the world of literature would deeply influence fellow playwrights and absurdist authors and, in turn, their many literary descendants. In this sense, Kierkegaard's legacy transcends the discipline of philosophy. It has found a home in existentialist and absurdist literature* with its self-consciously shared social, ideological, thematic, and formal elements.

Perhaps the most coherent discussions of Kierkegaard today come from the world of Protestant* academic and popular discourse. These thinkers—including people like the Anglican John Milbank,* Protestant scholar Stanley Hauerwas,* Scottish philosopher Alasdair MacIntyre,* and the late theologian Richard Neuhaus*—see Kierkegaard as an exemplary Christian thinker whose ideas speak to current problems of faith, modernity, society, and personal devotion.

NOTES

1   Howard and Edna Hong, introduction to *Fear and Trembling/Repetition* by Søren Kierkegaard (Princeton: Princeton University Press, 1983), xxxi.

2   See Søren Kierkegaard, *Either/Or*, trans. Howard and Edna Hong (Princeton: Princeton University Press, 1987).

3   Jacques Derrida, *The Gift of Death*, trans. David Wills (Chicago: University of Chicago Press, 1995).

4   Michael Weston, "Philosophy Always Comes Too Late: Lévinas and Kierkegaard," in *Kierkegaard and Modern Continental Philosophy: An Introduction* (London: Routledge, 1994); and John D. Caputo, *How to Read Kierkegaard* (New York: WW Norton, 2007), 55.

MODULE 11
IMPACT AND INFLUENCE TODAY

KEY POINTS

- *Fear and Trembling* remains a popular philosophical text that is also relevant to religious and theological studies.

- The book still challenges complacency and looks at the real or potential threat of an institutionalized Christianity* divorced from personal faith and obedience.

- New generations of scholars have explored the literary dimensions of Kierkegaard's work and have applied *Fear and Trembling's* assessments to contemporary society.

Position

More than 170 years after its publication, Søren Kierkegaard's *Fear and Trembling* still challenges conventional notions of ethics* and responsibility. The anxiety and hope Abraham* experienced remain universal human emotions, as scholars in the fields of philosophy and theology have recognized time and again. Kierkegaard's insistence on the individual's decisive and personal act of sacrifice is a timeless criticism of blind obedience to social norms. A 2013 conference in honor of the 200th anniversary of Kierkegaard's birth demonstrated that *Fear and Trembling* can also speak to issues of contemporary culture and the power of individual choice, addressing such twenty-first-century concerns as mass consumerism.

Many of Kierkegaard's contemporary readers identify as Christians. His thinking remains particularly pertinent in Western discussions about the state, the Church, and the social role of Christianity. Contemporary scholars have argued that Kierkegaard's concept of "Christendom"* can exist even in the absence of a state

66 *Fear and Trembling* continues to haunt us like no other of his writings. Its defense of individual existence still resonates at the end of a century marked by horrifying mass movements, while its depiction of radical religious obedience stirs new fears as we enter a period when older political ideologies are being replaced by renewed expressions of religious absolutism. **99**

Ronald Green, *The Cambridge Companion to Kierkegaard*

Church—as long as religious institutions shortchange the message of Christ.

Non-Christian readers of *Fear and Trembling*, such as feminist and literary theorist Julia Kristeva,* incorporate Kierkegaard's ideas into poststructuralist* (looking for meaning beyond the obvious narrative) analyses of social relations. Some have argued that in attempting to apply Kierkegaard outside of Christianity, she has lost some of his message. But we can still find an authentic trace of Kierkegaardian thought in her work.[1]

Interaction

Kierkegaard's writings have had the greatest influence on scholars and religious figures, including dissidents and activists. Arguably the most famous of these remains the German theologian Dietrich Bonhoeffer.* Kierkegaard's rejection of both popular views of what religion was and bourgeois* morality provided the religious inspiration for Bonhoeffer's plot to assassinate Hitler* during World War II.* Bonhoeffer considered Kierkegaard one of the great Christian thinkers, alongside sixteenth-century religious dissident Martin Luther* and the twentieth-century theologian Karl Barth.*

People outside academia know Kierkegaard as an existentialist.*[2]

But the title hardly does justice to Kierkegaard's vast body of work. Nor does it acknowledge his remarkable stylistic and formal innovations. His complex use of pseudonyms* and competing narrators represents one of the great examples of authorial multi-voicedness,* a notion American and European scholars have paid increasing attention to since the 1980s.[3]

The Continuing Debate

How much does *Fear and Trembling* disprove the works of Kierkegaard's predecessors and how much does it make use of them?[4] Scholars continue to debate this question today.

While *Fear and Trembling* most explicitly engages with G. W. F. Hegel,* serious scholarship has pointed to other influences as well. Moreover, for philosophers today *Fear and Trembling* serves more as a starting point for inquiry than as an element within a larger Idealist* debate.

The ancient Greek philosopher Socrates* was a major influence on Kierkegaard. Scholars have not devoted as much energy to investigating the Socratic dimension of *Fear and Trembling* as they have to exploring this influence in his other works.[5] Kierkegaard also adopted a variation of Plato's* technique of dialogues. This, too, deserves further study. The recent appreciation of Kierkegaard's talent as a stylist has given him an unexpected new life in the field of literary studies. Now scholars look at *Fear and Trembling* and his other works through the lenses of contemporary literary and cultural theory on authorship and the use of multiple voices.

Kierkegaard was very much aware of the way his narrators or pseudonyms allowed him to distance himself from the ideas put forward in his works. He would arguably welcome contemporary literary studies of his works as a complement to philosophical criticism.[6]

NOTES

1   Edward F. Mooney, "On Faith, the Maternal, and Postmodernism," in *Excursions with Kierkegaard: Others, Goods, Death, and Final Faith* (London: Bloomsbury, 2013).

2   The term "existential" became canonized with Sartre, but scholars often identify earlier thinkers such as Kierkegaard and Nietzsche as "existentialists" based on their ideas and not on any formal involvement with a group. One eminent scholar of existentialism, Walter Kaufmann, defined it as "not a philosophy but a label for several widely different revolts against traditional philosophy." See Walter Kaufmann, ed., *Existentialism from Dostoevsky to Sartre* (New York: Penguin, 1975), 11.

3   With the discovery of Mikhail Bakhtin (Russian philosopher and literary theorist) in the West in the 1980s, scholars such as Julia Kristeva were quick to see the similarities between Kierkegaard's use of authorial personas and Bakhtin's theory of polyphony, or multi-voicedness, in the novel.

4   For a discussion of the role of Kant, Hegel, and other important German philosophers in Kierkegaard's thought, see Clare Carlisle, *Kierkegaard's* Fear and Trembling*: A Reader's Guide* (New York: Continuum, 2010), 175.

5   Michael Weston, *Kierkegaard and Modern Continental Philosophy: An Introduction* (London: Routledge, 1994), 11–16.

6   In his journals, Kierkegaard wrote about pseudonymous poetic voices in his own work as means of "imaginary construction" that he preferred to the "historical-actual." See Howard and Edna Hong, introduction to *Fear and Trembling/Repetition* by Søren Kierkegaard (Princeton: Princeton University Press, 1983), xxiv.

MODULE 12
WHERE NEXT?

KEY POINTS

- *Fear and Trembling* has long been recognized as a foundational text for understanding Kierkegaard. Its impact is growing, not diminishing, with further study.

- Scholars agree that the text is very complex, with many layers of meaning and possible interpretation, inviting contemporary readers to continue to struggle to make sense of it.

- This seminal text challenges long-established philosophical archetypes.* It also offers a constructive vision for living—in both Kierkegaard's age and our own.

Potential

Students of Søren Kierkegaard continue to engage with the difficult question at the heart of *Fear and Trembling*: is there a conflict between ethics* and religion? This central question leads to others: Must there always be opposition between the ethical life* and the religious life? Or is it something that secular, non-religious, or modern society can solve or has solved? Can the individual have a responsibility that transcends ethics and does *not* involve religion? Today's readers also see the work as a critique of materialism and consumerism—the modern equivalents of the aesthetic life* of pleasure Kierkegaard attacked throughout his early works.[1]

Kierkegaard's compelling prose and the relatively short length of many of his works, including *Fear and Trembling*, make his writing highly accessible to undergraduates. His semi-tragic life story—a man who sacrificed the woman he loved and died young at the age of just 42—also captures the modern imagination.

❝ Fear and Trembling has earned renown as a provocative statement of challenge. But it is far more than that. Fear and Trembling is an introduction or propaedeutic to Kierkegaard's authorship as a whole. Read at all the levels of its meaning, Fear and Trembling contains the major themes of Christian faith and ethics that will emerge in the ensuing pseudonymous works and many of the religious discourses. ❞

Ronald Green, *The Cambridge Companion to Kierkegaard*

Kierkegaard himself anticipated the lasting impact that *Fear and Trembling* would have, saying it was "enough for an imperishable name as an author."[2]

Future Directions

Current supporters of Søren Kierkegaard's *Fear and Trembling* generally fall into three major camps. While not mutually exclusive, these "camps" demonstrate the central spheres in which Kierkegaard continues to influence contemporary thought.

The first camp, at least in the Western world, consists primarily of academics focusing on the influence, content, and reception of *Fear and Trembling*. These include the scholars and biographers Bruce Kirmmse,* Alastair Hannay,* and Howard and Edna Hong.* Recognizing *Fear and Trembling* as a significant work in Kierkegaard's canon, these scholars try to uncover alternate readings or new nuances in the text. To some extent they oppose or extend older debates about the meaning of the text and the debt it owes to older philosophers like Hegel,* Kant,* or Schelling.* Scholars in this camp use the text to improve their knowledge of Kierkegaard's work, rather than as a tool for ideological or personal agendas.

In the second camp, academic and popular theologians use Kierkegaard to interpret and assess theological concepts, to study the Bible's* text closely and to inform their view of modern Christian* society. Theologians such as John Milbank,* a popular Anglican* thinker, and the American Stanley Hauerwas* combine academic rigor with pointed social and religious concerns when they discuss *Fear and Trembling*.

Milbank* rejects modernist* and secular ways of reading, interpreting, and disseminating knowledge, and he sees the seeds of his position in *Fear and Trembling*. Because Milbank's radical orthodoxy* (placing theology rather than science at the center of the pursuit of knowledge and truth) borrows much from post-World War II* theologian Karl Barth,* one can read a Kierkegaardian thread woven throughout a debate on the response of Christianity to modernism.[3] While Kierkegaard certainly intended *Fear and Trembling* to have practical applications in the life of his reader, it is still difficult to know how much he would have sympathized with the politics of Milbank and his specific project of rejecting modernity and secular scholarship—or indeed with Anglicanism.

In the third camp, scholars of literary theory have become interested in *Fear and Trembling* and other complex works Kierkegaard wrote under pseudonyms* for their use of literary devices. In a 2015 study of *Fear and Trembling*,[4] a range of Kierkegaard scholars including British professor and Kierkegaard translator Alastair Hannay explore the interplay of literary, rhetorical,* and philosophical themes in Kierkegaard's writing. While literary theorists took almost a century to embrace *Fear and Trembling*, they arguably offer a more faithful reading of the text than many earlier scholars, who ignored or dismissed questions of authorship and form. But eager to deconstruct* the works and create poststructuralist* readings—and lacking theological training—literary theorists tend to avoid the philosophical and metaphysical questions of the text. And, for Kierkegaard, these questions lay at the heart of his work.

Summary

In *Fear and Trembling,* Søren Kierkegaard created a work of great learning, philosophical insight, religious conviction, and literary sophistication. It is representative of Kierkegaard's thinking, in terms of both its content and the work's unique literary execution. *Fear and Trembling* demonstrates his concern with the individual's potential to live a life of resignation,* hope, and obedience to a God who, paradoxically as it may seem in light of human suffering, is love.

Kierkegaard has left an indelible mark on Western philosophy, profoundly shifting the discussions even today. In rejecting universals and wholly rational systems of philosophy, he predicts the twentieth-century revolts that developed against Hegel and Kant. His disapproval of the established Church and of the mediocrity of popular piety has inspired Christians and non-Christians alike to search for authentic living. His criticisms of individuals who set their course solely by the standards of society continue to influence intellectual conversations in the United States and Europe.

Ultimately, Kierkegaard wrote *Fear and Trembling* to challenge the way in which a given individual can live his life. This organizing idea makes the work timeless. *Fear and Trembling* offers insight to readers across generations and cultures. As Kierkegaard expected, it has created lasting fame for him and his ideas.

NOTES

1   Kierkegaard proposes that people often live in three primary ways: the aesthetic, the ethical, and the religious. The aesthete lives for himself and for pleasure and entertainment, and would today be considered someone enthralled with consumerism. In *Fear and Trembling* Kierkegaard proposes a higher way of living, with Abraham as the model.

2   Howard and Edna Hong, introduction to *Fear and Trembling/Repetition* by Søren Kierkegaard (Princeton: Princeton University Press, 1983), xxxiv.

3   John Milbank, "The Sublime in Kierkegaard," *The Heythrop Journal* 37, no. 3 (1996): 298–321.

4   Daniel Conway, ed., *Kierkegaard's* Fear and Trembling*: A Critical Guide* (Cambridge: Cambridge University Press, 2015).

GLOSSARIES

GLOSSARY OF TERMS

Absurdist literature: writing that is fantastical and grotesque or has illogical plot developments that often satirize or criticize modern society, politics, and culture.

Aesthetic life: For Kierkegaard, people can have different fundamental orientations for their life: aesthetic, ethical,* or religious. The aesthetic life is concerned with beauty, as well as pleasure and sensory experience.

Allegory: a narrative (in prose or poem) that can be interpreted as having a hidden meaning beneath the obvious, literal meaning.

Anglicanism: a form of Protestant* Christianity that closely resembles Roman Catholicism. Anglicanism is the Christianity practiced by the Church of England, and is known in the United States as Episcopalianism.

Archetypes: In philosophy, an archetype is a Platonic idea of a pure form that embodies the fundamental characteristics of a thing.

The Binding of Isaac: Chapter 22 in the Book of Genesis* (in the Christian tradition's Old Testament)* tells the story of the binding of Isaac. Isaac is the only legitimate son of Abraham,* an old man who has been promised by God that his offspring will become a great nation. In this episode God tells Abraham he must sacrifice his only son as an offering. Although this would seem to destroy Abraham's chance of becoming the father of a nation, he nonetheless obeys God, takes his son up to Mount Moriah, ties him up, and prepares to kill him. However, at the last moment an angel stops Abraham, saying that now God knows Abraham truly fears God, God will spare Isaac. Abraham sacrifices a male sheep instead and God renews his promise to make Abraham the father of many.

Book of Genesis: the first book of the Old Testament (for Christians), or the first book of the Torah (for Jews*). It tells the story of the creation of the world and the establishment of the Hebrew people as the chosen people of God.

Bourgeois: denotes middle class, but derogatorily implies middle-class anxieties about wealth, proper behavior, and social standing.

Christianity: a major religion based on the life and teachings of Jesus Christ in the first century C.E.

Christendom: a term often used to denote the institution of Christianity, largely in the sense that the Church is a political actor. Christendom is represented by institutional figures and structures such as popes, hierarchies, and alliances with secular powers.

Civil disobedience: the conscious refusal to follow unjust laws on the basis that it is more just to break unjust laws than to obey them. Civil disobedience was an important part of protest movements in Europe, America, and India in the twentieth century.

Continental philosophy: an umbrella term for nineteenth- and twentieth-century nonanalytic European philosophy.

Deconstructionist: refers to the philosophy or literary method of deconstructionism. Deconstructionism claims that meanings and philosophies can be taken apart and exposed as unstable.

Devotional: refers to the religious or spiritual life, specifically in terms of being used for worship or spiritual growth.

Ecclesiology: the theological study of the Christian Church, often with an emphasis on the role of the Church in mankind's relationship to God and to salvation.

Epoch: a synonym for era, age, or time period.

Ethical life: For Kierkegaard, people can have different fundamental orientations for their life: aesthetic,* ethical, or religious. The ethical life is the life concerned with following moral and ethical rules and standards.

Ethics: the moral principles that organize human behavior. Ethics can also refer to the study of these principles and how the principles are applied in various situations.

Existentialism: a type of philosophy or literature that values the individual's wholly unique experience of life as a thinking, feeling subject who must make sense of a difficult or senseless world.

Hegelian: a person who or philosophy that follows the nineteenth-century German philosopher G. W. F. Hegel. Hegelian often refers specifically to Hegel's idea of history as continuous cycle of opposing forces or ideas that encounter, resist, and eventually resolve themselves (dialectics).

Idealist: Idealist describes philosophies that claim that reality is fundamentally mental, or understood mentally, rather than materially.

Institutional Christianity: refers to the organized structure of Christianity with pastors, bishops, committees, and official state relations. Kierkegaard saw the message of Christianity as being at odds with its institutional and cultural trappings.

Judaism: a religion believing in one God that originated in the Middle East and traces its beginnings back three thousand years. Christianity emerged from one of the many different Jewish movements that existed in the first century C.E.

Jews: members of the Jewish faith, Judaism.*

Knight of faith: Kierkegaard introduces the idea of "knight of faith," someone whose faith in God allows him or her to survive trials and hardships. To become a "knight of faith," one must renounce one's personal desires and retain hope.

Mauvaise foi: Existentialist philosophers used this French term that literally means "bad faith" to describe rationality. Rationality is a bad faith because it tries to impose order on a world that is chaotic and irrational.

Melancholy: also called melancholia, an ancient concept that survives into modern times and describes the state of feeling sad with no clear reason.

Merman: a mythical creature that is half-man and half-fish. European fairy tales feature mermen and one such story appears in *Fear and Trembling.*

Modernist: refers to anything related to modernity, or the era of Western civilization after the Renaissance and up to the twentieth century.

Multi-voicedness: This term refers to texts that offer multiple authorial perspectives; specifically, those texts in which it is impossible to tell which, if any, of these multiple voices is the most authoritative, rendering all of the voices equally important.

Nazis: The German political party founded by Adolf Hitler in 1919. Nazi is short for *Nationalsozialismus* (National Socialism). The party controlled Germany (and increasingly large parts of Europe) until the end of World War II in 1945.

Noumena: the plural form of the Greek *noumenon*. Plato* conceived of *noumena* as things that are known without reference to the senses. In other words, ideas—as opposed to things we must use the senses to know, like things in the physical world.

Old Testament: The Christian Bible is composed of two parts: the Old Testament and the New Testament. The Old Testament is the name for the collection of writings that are sacred to the Jewish faith (known by Jews as the Tanakh) that are a part of the Christian faith as well.

Political-ecclesiastical: refers to the political power of the institutional Church. Ecclesiastical refers to the institution of the Church or its clergy.

Postmodern: refers to anything related to the reaction against modernism in the twentieth century. Often, the term carries the connotation of being self-referential, absurd, or anti-rational.

Poststructuralism: a movement in the mid- to late-twentieth century that aimed to "destabilize" texts by looking for meaning beyond the obvious narratives or context.

Problemata: the Greek term for problem that is sometimes used in philosophical debates and conversations for the systematic consideration of problems and solutions in reference to an intellectual investigation.

Protestantism: one of the three major branches of Christianity (along with Roman Catholicism and Orthodoxy). Beginning as a movement under Martin Luther* in the sixteenth century, it has spread in diverse forms throughout the world.

Pseudonym: a false name, or pen name, used by an author in their writings.

Pseudonymous: "false named," it describes the title or name a person chooses to use in place of his or her own name.

Radical orthodoxy: a theological movement that attempts to place theology rather than science at the center of the intellectual pursuit of knowledge and truth. It aims to critique secularism and modernism in particular.

Remainder: Remaindered books are titles that have not sold well, so the publisher sells the remaining copies at a very low price.

Renunciation: the complete rejection of something, normally a belief or plan of action. It can refer particularly to an act of rejection that doesn't replace the belief or plan with something else.

***Repetition*:** a work by Kierkegaard published simultaneously with *Fear and Trembling*. The work questions repetition and memory, specifically in the context of a young man who has proposed to a woman but has changed his mind about marriage.

Resignation: the acceptance of something undesirable. Often it refers to accepting something negative that is out of your control or inevitable.

Rhetorical: refers to rhetoric, which is the art of speaking or writing convincingly.

Systematic philosophy: the work of Hegel and Kant gave rise to attempts to offer systematic philosophy, that is, a system of philosophical claims and arguments that could address every aspect of human cognition, behavior, society, and morality.

Teleological: means that something is destined or ultimately meant for a certain goal or aim. The "teleological suspension of the ethical" is the notion that one can, in a certain instance, act contrary to common ethical standards for the sake of something greater.

Transcendence: a concept in philosophy for the act (often mental or spiritual) of going beyond normal experience. This can mean experiencing something supernatural, unnatural, or beyond normal human comprehension.

World War I (1914–18): an international conflict centered in Europe and involving the major economic world powers of the day.

World War II (1939–45): a global conflict fought between the Axis Powers (Germany, Italy, and Japan) and the victorious Allied Powers (the United Kingdom and its colonies, the Soviet Union, and the United States).

PEOPLE MENTIONED IN THE TEXT

Abraham is a figure in the Old Testament* of the Bible. He was the father of the Jewish nation.

Karl Barth (1886–1968) was a Swiss Protestant* systematic theologian. Barth was one of the most prolific theologians of the twentieth century and undertook the enormous project of attempting to develop a systematic theology for the postwar epoch.

Dietrich Bonhoeffer (1906–45) was a celebrated German pastor, theologian, and political dissident. He was arrested for an attempted assassination plot against Hitler* in 1943 and was executed by the Nazis* in 1945.

Albert Camus (1913–60) was an important twentieth-century French (Algerian-born) philosopher and author of fiction. Camus's works explored the absurd, nihilism, the importance of the individual, and freedom.

Johannes Climacus is the pseudonymous* author of Kierkegaard's *Philosophical Fragments* and *Concluding Unscientific Postscript to Philosophical Fragments,* as well as an unpublished work entitled *Johannes Climacus, or De omnibus dubitandum est.*

Constantine Constantius is the pseudonymous author of Kierkegaard's *Repetition** and selections from *Stages on Life's Way.*

Jacques Derrida (1930–2004) was an influential French (Algerian-born) literary theorist who spent much of his career in the United States. His work fundamentally shaped the schools we now call postmodernism,* poststructuralism,* and deconstructionism.*

Johannes de Silentio was the pseudonym under which Kierkegaard published *Fear and Trembling*. It is Latin for "John the Silent."

Magnús Eiríksson (1806–81) was an Icelandic theologian and a contemporary of Kierkegaard. His writings criticized Church dogmas, especially the divinity of Jesus Christ. He published under the pseudonym Theophilius Nicolaus.

Mohandas K. Gandhi (1869–1948), also known by the honorific "Mahatma" (meaning "venerable"), led the movement seeking India's independence from Britain. He practiced nonviolent resistance and urged his followers to do the same. He was assassinated, and his birthday is celebrated as a national holiday in India and internationally as a Day of Nonviolence.

Ronald Green is an American professor of religion. His work focuses on ethics* and contemporary issues (legal, biomedical, and so on), as well as the philosophy of ethics.

Johann Gottlieb Fichte (1762–1814) was a German philosopher. Fichte's work on self-consciousness and self-awareness represent a transition in German Idealism between the thoughts of Kant* and Hegel.*

Alastair Hannay (born 1932) is a British thinker and professor emeritus at the University of Oslo. He has translated Kierkegaard and written an intellectual biography and a treatise about him.

Stanley Hauerwas (born 1940) is an American professor, ethicist, and theologian. He has contributed a great deal of work on theology, political theology, and ethics, and his outspoken criticism of American civil religion echoes Kierkegaard's own concerns.

G. W .F. Hegel (1770–1831) was a highly prolific and influential German philosopher. His deeply idealist* and historical views of the world shaped German and then European philosophy.

Johan Heiberg (1791–1860) was a Danish writer and thinker. He is best known for his work as a poet, playwright, and literary critic, although he also studied Hegelian philosophy.

Martin Heidegger (1889–1976) was a German philosopher who made highly influential contributions to phenomenology—a philosophical movement that studies experience and consciousness; ontology—the study of the nature of being; and existentialism.* His most celebrated work is *Being and Time* (*Sein und Zeit* in German), published in 1927. Heidegger was influenced by Nietzsche and Kant, and his work would have an enormous impact on Jean-Paul Sartre and Jacques Derrida, among many others.

Adolf Hitler (1889–1945) was the chancellor and then leader of Germany from 1933 until his death in 1945. He led Germany in an attempt to take over Europe and his ideology was based on ideas of German political, cultural, and racial superiority.

Edna Hong (1913–2007) was an American scholar and translator, who translated numerous works by Kierkegaard from Danish to English alongside her husband, Howard.

Howard Hong (1912–2010) was a scholar and translator who taught Kierkegaard to students for more than 40 years. Along with his wife, Edna, he translated numerous works by Kierkegaard from Danish to English.

Karl Jaspers (1883–1969) was a German psychiatrist and philosopher. His work is influential at the intersection of theology, psychiatry, and philosophy and has been linked to existentialism.

Immanuel Kant (1724–1804) was a Prussian philosopher who revolutionized German thought. He is best known for his works on reason, morality, and the nature of reality and his proposal of an absolute system of ethics.

Martin Luther King, Jr. (1929–68) was a Baptist minister and leader of the American Civil Rights movement that sought full legal equality for African Americans. His embrace of nonviolent resistance, even in the face of great brutality by opponents of civil rights, won him the Nobel Peace Prize in 1964. He was assassinated and his birthday is celebrated as a national holiday in the United States.

Bruce Kirmmse is an American scholar and translator. He has written extensively on Kierkegaard and translated secondary literature on Kierkegaard from Danish into English.

Julia Kristeva (born 1941) is a Bulgarian-French philosopher, literary critic, psychoanalyst, sociologist, and novelist. She is known for her pioneering works on literature, linguistics, cultural theory, and feminism.

Emmanuel Lévinas (1906–95) was a French Jewish philosopher. His career focused on ethics, existentialism, and Jewish philosophy.

Walter Lowrie (1868–1959) was an American clergyman and scholar. He is best known for his translations of Kierkegaard and for writings on Kierkegaard's theology.

Martin Luther (1483–1546) was a German friar, priest, and professor of theology. Luther rejected certain teachings and practices of the Roman Catholic Church and started what is now called the Protestant Reformation.

Alasdair MacIntyre (born 1929) is a Scottish philosopher. He is best known for his works on theology, as well as moral and political philosophy. He enjoyed a long teaching career in the United Kingdom and United States.

Hans Lassen Martensen (1808–84) was a Danish theologian and academic. Kierkegaard clashed with him over Martensen's eulogy for Bishop Jacob Mynster.

John Milbank (born 1952) is a British theologian and professor. He is one of the founders of the Radical Orthodoxy movement, a theological movement that places theology rather than science at the center of the intellectual pursuit of knowledge and truth.

Jacob P. Mynster (1775–1854) was a Danish theologian and one of the bishops of Denmark in 1834–54. Kierkegaard criticized Mynster in his writings.

Richard Neuhaus (1936–2009) was a prominent Christian thinker who converted to Roman Catholicism from Lutheranism. He was the founder and editor of the Roman Catholic journal *First Things* and author of many books on religious and theological issues.

Theophilius Nicolaus was the alias of Magnús Eiríksson, an Icelandic theologian who spent most of his life in Copenhagen. Nicolaus was critical of Church dogma and disliked speculative theology.

Friedrich Nietzsche (1844–1900) was a German philosopher and cultural critic who was deeply critical of any organized religions or belief systems because, among other things, he believed they were repressive and made apologies for the weak. In contrast to the weak or self-sacrificing, Nietzsche developed his idea of the *Übermensch* or "superman."

Regine Olsen (1822–1904) was a Danish woman whom Kierkegaard loved. After he broke off their engagement suddenly, she eventually married her tutor, Johan Frederik Schlegel. After Schlegel's death in 1867, she began speaking to Kierkegaard biographers about their relationship.

Saint Paul (c.4–c.64 c.e.) also known as Paul the Apostle, was an early Christian convert from Judaism. He wrote a number of the texts that are now part of the New Testament and is an enormously important figure and thinker in Christianity.

Plato (c.425–348 b.c.e.) was a Greek philosopher whose teachings, written in the form of dialogues, are seen by many as the cornerstones of Western thought.

Jean-Paul Sartre (1905–80) was a French existentialist philosopher, author, activist, and literary critic. He was one of the most influential figures in twentieth-century French philosophy and Marxism.

Friedrich Schelling (1775–1854) was a German philosopher and contemporary and friend of Hegel. Schelling was an idealist, like Hegel, but his philosophical system was less exhaustive than his colleague's.

Carl Schmitt (1888–1985) was a German philosopher and political theorist. Schmitt contributed to twentieth-century legal and political theory, particularly in discussions about the nature and implementation of political power.

Socrates (c. 469–399 B.C.E.) was a Greek philosopher and teacher of Plato. All his writings come to us as recorded by other people, and are foundational texts of Western philosophy.

WORKS CITED

WORKS CITED

Caputo, John D. *How to Read Kierkegaard*. New York: WW Norton, 2007.

Carlisle, Clare. *Kierkegaard's Fear and Trembling*. New York: Continuum, 2010.

Conway, Daniel, ed. *Kierkegaard's* Fear and Trembling: *A Critical Guide*. Cambridge: Cambridge University Press, 2015.

Derrida, Jacques. *The Gift of Death*. Translated by David Wills. Chicago: University of Chicago Press, 1995.

Garff, Joakim. *Søren Kierkegaard: A Biography*. Translated by Bruce H. Kirmmse. Princeton: Princeton University Press, 2007.

Hannay, Alastair. *Kierkegaard: A Biography*. Cambridge: Cambridge University Press, 2003.

Hannay, Alastair, and Gordon D. Marino (eds). *The Cambridge Companion to Kierkegaard*. Cambridge: Cambridge University Press, 1998.

Hegel, Georg Wilhelm Fredrich. *Elements of the Philosophy of Right.* Translated by H. B. Nisbet. Cambridge: Cambridge University Press, 1991.

Inwood, Michael, ed. "Inner and Outer, Internal and External." In *A Hegel Dictionary* (Blackwell Publishing, Blackwell Reference Online). Accessed April 13, 2015. www.blackwellreference.com/subscriber/tocnode. html?id=g9780631175339_chunk_g978063117533913_ss1-9.

Kant, Immanuel. *The Conflict of the Faculties*. Translated by Mary J. Gregor. Lincoln: University of Nebraska Press, 1992.

——. *Critique of Pure Reason.* Translated by Werner Pluhar. Indianapolis: Hackett Publishing Co., 1996.

Kaufmann, Walter. *Existentialism from Dostoevsky to Sartre.* New York: Penguin, 1975.

Kierkegaard, Søren. *The Concept of Anxiety*. Translated by Reidar Thomte. Princeton: Princeton University Press, 1981.

——. *Concluding Unscientific Postscript to Philosophical Fragments.* Translated by Howard and Edna Hong. Princeton: Princeton University Press, 1992.

——. *Eighteen Upbuilding Discourses.* Translated by Howard Hong and Edna Hong. Princeton: Princeton University Press, 1990.

——. *Either/Or.* Translated by Howard and Edna Hong. Princeton: Princeton University Press, 1987.

Macat Analysis of **Søren Kierkegaard's** *Fear and Trembling*

——. *Fear and Trembling/Repetition*. Translated by Howard and Edna Hong. Princeton: Princeton University Press, 1983.

——. *The Moment and Late Writings.* Translated by Howard and Edna Hong. Princeton: Princeton University Press, 2009.

——. *Philosophical Fragments*. Translated by Howard and Edna Hong. Princeton: Princeton University Press, 1985.

——. *The Sickness unto Death.* Translated by Howard and Edna Hong. Princeton: Princeton University Press, 1983.

——. *Stages on Life's Way*. Translated by Howard and Edna Hong. Princeton: Princeton University Press, 1988.

McBride, William. "Sartre's Debts to Kierkegaard: A Partial Reckoning." In Martin J. Matustik and Merold Westphal (eds), *Kierkegaard in Post/Modernity*, 18–42. Bloomington and Indianapolis: Indiana University Press, 1995.

Milbank, John, "The Sublime in Kierkegaard." *The Heythrop Journal* 37, no. 3 (1996): 298–321.

Mooney, Edward F. *Excursions with Kierkegaard: Others, Goods, Death, and Final Faith*. London: Bloomsbury, 2013.

Sartre, Jean-Paul. *Being and Nothingness.* Translated by Hazel Barnes. New York: Washington Square Press, 1992.

Stewart, Jon, ed. *Kierkegaard's Influence on the Social Sciences*. Surrey: Ashgate, 2011.

——. *Kierkegaard's Influence on Theology: German Protestant Theology*. Farnham, Surrey: Ashgate Publishing, 2012.

Weston, Michael. *Kierkegaard and Modern Continental Philosophy: An Introduction*. London: Routledge, 1994.

88

THE MACAT LIBRARY
BY DISCIPLINE

AFRICANA STUDIES

Chinua Achebe's *An Image of Africa: Racism in Conrad's Heart of Darkness*
W. E. B. Du Bois's *The Souls of Black Folk*
Zora Neale Huston's *Characteristics of Negro Expression*
Martin Luther King Jr's *Why We Can't Wait*
Toni Morrison's *Playing in the Dark: Whiteness in the American Literary Imagination*

ANTHROPOLOGY

Arjun Appadurai's *Modernity at Large: Cultural Dimensions of Globalisation*
Philippe Ariès's *Centuries of Childhood*
Franz Boas's *Race, Language and Culture*
Kim Chan & Renée Mauborgne's *Blue Ocean Strategy*
Jared Diamond's *Guns, Germs & Steel: the Fate of Human Societies*
Jared Diamond's *Collapse: How Societies Choose to Fail or Survive*
E. E. Evans-Pritchard's *Witchcraft, Oracles and Magic Among the Azande*
James Ferguson's *The Anti-Politics Machine*
Clifford Geertz's *The Interpretation of Cultures*
David Graeber's *Debt: the First 5000 Years*
Karen Ho's *Liquidated: An Ethnography of Wall Street*
Geert Hofstede's *Culture's Consequences: Comparing Values, Behaviors, Institutes and Organizations across Nations*
Claude Lévi-Strauss's *Structural Anthropology*
Jay Macleod's *Ain't No Makin' It: Aspirations and Attainment in a Low-Income Neighborhood*
Saba Mahmood's *The Politics of Piety: The Islamic Revival and the Feminist Subject*
Marcel Mauss's *The Gift*

BUSINESS

Jean Lave & Etienne Wenger's *Situated Learning*
Theodore Levitt's *Marketing Myopia*
Burton G. Malkiel's *A Random Walk Down Wall Street*
Douglas McGregor's *The Human Side of Enterprise*
Michael Porter's *Competitive Strategy: Creating and Sustaining Superior Performance*
John Kotter's *Leading Change*
C. K. Prahalad & Gary Hamel's *The Core Competence of the Corporation*

CRIMINOLOGY

Michelle Alexander's *The New Jim Crow: Mass Incarceration in the Age of Colorblindness*
Michael R. Gottfredson & Travis Hirschi's *A General Theory of Crime*
Richard Herrnstein & Charles A. Murray's *The Bell Curve: Intelligence and Class Structure in American Life*
Elizabeth Loftus's *Eyewitness Testimony*
Jay Macleod's *Ain't No Makin' It: Aspirations and Attainment in a Low-Income Neighborhood*
Philip Zimbardo's *The Lucifer Effect*

ECONOMICS

Janet Abu-Lughod's *Before European Hegemony*
Ha-Joon Chang's *Kicking Away the Ladder*
David Brion Davis's *The Problem of Slavery in the Age of Revolution*
Milton Friedman's *The Role of Monetary Policy*
Milton Friedman's *Capitalism and Freedom*
David Graeber's *Debt: the First 5000 Years*
Friedrich Hayek's *The Road to Serfdom*
Karen Ho's *Liquidated: An Ethnography of Wall Street*

John Maynard Keynes's *The General Theory of Employment, Interest and Money*
Charles P. Kindleberger's *Manias, Panics and Crashes*
Robert Lucas's *Why Doesn't Capital Flow from Rich to Poor Countries?*
Burton G. Malkiel's *A Random Walk Down Wall Street*
Thomas Robert Malthus's *An Essay on the Principle of Population*
Karl Marx's *Capital*
Thomas Piketty's *Capital in the Twenty-First Century*
Amartya Sen's *Development as Freedom*
Adam Smith's *The Wealth of Nations*
Nassim Nicholas Taleb's *The Black Swan: The Impact of the Highly Improbable*
Amos Tversky's & Daniel Kahneman's *Judgment under Uncertainty: Heuristics and Biases*
Mahbub Ul Haq's *Reflections on Human Development*
Max Weber's *The Protestant Ethic and the Spirit of Capitalism*

FEMINISM AND GENDER STUDIES

Judith Butler's *Gender Trouble*
Simone De Beauvoir's *The Second Sex*
Michel Foucault's *History of Sexuality*
Betty Friedan's *The Feminine Mystique*
Saba Mahmood's *The Politics of Piety: The Islamic Revival and the Feminist Subject*
Joan Wallach Scott's *Gender and the Politics of History*
Mary Wollstonecraft's *A Vindication of the Rights of Woman*
Virginia Woolf's *A Room of One's Own*

GEOGRAPHY

The Brundtland Report's *Our Common Future*
Rachel Carson's *Silent Spring*
Charles Darwin's *On the Origin of Species*
James Ferguson's *The Anti-Politics Machine*
Jane Jacobs's *The Death and Life of Great American Cities*
James Lovelock's *Gaia: A New Look at Life on Earth*
Amartya Sen's *Development as Freedom*
Mathis Wackernagel & William Rees's *Our Ecological Footprint*

HISTORY

Janet Abu-Lughod's *Before European Hegemony*
Benedict Anderson's *Imagined Communities*
Bernard Bailyn's *The Ideological Origins of the American Revolution*
Hanna Batatu's *The Old Social Classes And The Revolutionary Movements Of Iraq*
Christopher Browning's *Ordinary Men: Reserve Police Batallion 101 and the Final Solution in Poland*
Edmund Burke's *Reflections on the Revolution in France*
William Cronon's *Nature's Metropolis: Chicago And The Great West*
Alfred W. Crosby's *The Columbian Exchange*
Hamid Dabashi's *Iran: A People Interrupted*
David Brion Davis's *The Problem of Slavery in the Age of Revolution*
Nathalie Zemon Davis's *The Return of Martin Guerre*
Jared Diamond's *Guns, Germs & Steel: the Fate of Human Societies*
Frank Dikotter's *Mao's Great Famine*
John W Dower's *War Without Mercy: Race And Power In The Pacific War*
W. E. B. Du Bois's *The Souls of Black Folk*
Richard J. Evans's *In Defence of History*
Lucien Febvre's *The Problem of Unbelief in the 16th Century*
Sheila Fitzpatrick's *Everyday Stalinism*

The Macat Library By Discipline

Eric Foner's *Reconstruction: America's Unfinished Revolution, 1863-1877*
Michel Foucault's *Discipline and Punish*
Michel Foucault's *History of Sexuality*
Francis Fukuyama's *The End of History and the Last Man*
John Lewis Gaddis's *We Now Know: Rethinking Cold War History*
Ernest Gellner's *Nations and Nationalism*
Eugene Genovese's *Roll, Jordan, Roll: The World the Slaves Made*
Carlo Ginzburg's *The Night Battles*
Daniel Goldhagen's *Hitler's Willing Executioners*
Jack Goldstone's *Revolution and Rebellion in the Early Modern World*
Antonio Gramsci's *The Prison Notebooks*
Alexander Hamilton, John Jay & James Madison's *The Federalist Papers*
Christopher Hill's *The World Turned Upside Down*
Carole Hillenbrand's *The Crusades: Islamic Perspectives*
Thomas Hobbes's *Leviathan*
Eric Hobsbawm's *The Age Of Revolution*
John A. Hobson's *Imperialism: A Study*
Albert Hourani's *History of the Arab Peoples*
Samuel P. Huntington's *The Clash of Civilizations and the Remaking of World Order*
C. L. R. James's *The Black Jacobins*
Tony Judt's *Postwar: A History of Europe Since 1945*
Ernst Kantorowicz's *The King's Two Bodies: A Study in Medieval Political Theology*
Paul Kennedy's *The Rise and Fall of the Great Powers*
Ian Kershaw's *The "Hitler Myth": Image and Reality in the Third Reich*
John Maynard Keynes's *The General Theory of Employment, Interest and Money*
Charles P. Kindleberger's *Manias, Panics and Crashes*
Martin Luther King Jr's *Why We Can't Wait*
Henry Kissinger's *World Order: Reflections on the Character of Nations and the Course of History*
Thomas Kuhn's *The Structure of Scientific Revolutions*
Georges Lefebvre's *The Coming of the French Revolution*
John Locke's *Two Treatises of Government*
Niccolò Machiavelli's *The Prince*
Thomas Robert Malthus's *An Essay on the Principle of Population*
Mahmood Mamdani's *Citizen and Subject: Contemporary Africa And The Legacy Of Late Colonialism*
Karl Marx's *Capital*
Stanley Milgram's *Obedience to Authority*
John Stuart Mill's *On Liberty*
Thomas Paine's *Common Sense*
Thomas Paine's *Rights of Man*
Geoffrey Parker's *Global Crisis: War, Climate Change and Catastrophe in the Seventeenth Century*
Jonathan Riley-Smith's *The First Crusade and the Idea of Crusading*
Jean-Jacques Rousseau's *The Social Contract*
Joan Wallach Scott's *Gender and the Politics of History*
Theda Skocpol's *States and Social Revolutions*
Adam Smith's *The Wealth of Nations*
Timothy Snyder's *Bloodlands: Europe Between Hitler and Stalin*
Sun Tzu's *The Art of War*
Keith Thomas's *Religion and the Decline of Magic*
Thucydides's *The History of the Peloponnesian War*
Frederick Jackson Turner's *The Significance of the Frontier in American History*
Odd Arne Westad's *The Global Cold War: Third World Interventions And The Making Of Our Times*

LITERATURE

Chinua Achebe's *An Image of Africa: Racism in Conrad's Heart of Darkness*
Roland Barthes's *Mythologies*
Homi K. Bhabha's *The Location of Culture*
Judith Butler's *Gender Trouble*
Simone De Beauvoir's *The Second Sex*
Ferdinand De Saussure's *Course in General Linguistics*
T. S. Eliot's *The Sacred Wood: Essays on Poetry and Criticism*
Zora Neale Huston's *Characteristics of Negro Expression*
Toni Morrison's *Playing in the Dark: Whiteness in the American Literary Imagination*
Edward Said's *Orientalism*
Gayatri Chakravorty Spivak's *Can the Subaltern Speak?*
Mary Wollstonecraft's *A Vindication of the Rights of Women*
Virginia Woolf's *A Room of One's Own*

PHILOSOPHY

Elizabeth Anscombe's *Modern Moral Philosophy*
Hannah Arendt's *The Human Condition*
Aristotle's *Metaphysics*
Aristotle's *Nicomachean Ethics*
Edmund Gettier's *Is Justified True Belief Knowledge?*
Georg Wilhelm Friedrich Hegel's *Phenomenology of Spirit*
David Hume's *Dialogues Concerning Natural Religion*
David Hume's *The Enquiry for Human Understanding*
Immanuel Kant's *Religion within the Boundaries of Mere Reason*
Immanuel Kant's *Critique of Pure Reason*
Søren Kierkegaard's *The Sickness Unto Death*
Søren Kierkegaard's *Fear and Trembling*
C. S. Lewis's *The Abolition of Man*
Alasdair MacIntyre's *After Virtue*
Marcus Aurelius's *Meditations*
Friedrich Nietzsche's *On the Genealogy of Morality*
Friedrich Nietzsche's *Beyond Good and Evil*
Plato's *Republic*
Plato's *Symposium*
Jean-Jacques Rousseau's *The Social Contract*
Gilbert Ryle's *The Concept of Mind*
Baruch Spinoza's *Ethics*
Sun Tzu's *The Art of War*
Ludwig Wittgenstein's *Philosophical Investigations*

POLITICS

Benedict Anderson's *Imagined Communities*
Aristotle's *Politics*
Bernard Bailyn's *The Ideological Origins of the American Revolution*
Edmund Burke's *Reflections on the Revolution in France*
John C. Calhoun's *A Disquisition on Government*
Ha-Joon Chang's *Kicking Away the Ladder*
Hamid Dabashi's *Iran: A People Interrupted*
Hamid Dabashi's *Theology of Discontent: The Ideological Foundation of the Islamic Revolution in Iran*
Robert Dahl's *Democracy and its Critics*
Robert Dahl's *Who Governs?*
David Brion Davis's *The Problem of Slavery in the Age of Revolution*

The Macat Library By Discipline

Alexis De Tocqueville's *Democracy in America*
James Ferguson's *The Anti-Politics Machine*
Frank Dikotter's *Mao's Great Famine*
Sheila Fitzpatrick's *Everyday Stalinism*
Eric Foner's *Reconstruction: America's Unfinished Revolution, 1863-1877*
Milton Friedman's *Capitalism and Freedom*
Francis Fukuyama's *The End of History and the Last Man*
John Lewis Gaddis's *We Now Know: Rethinking Cold War History*
Ernest Gellner's *Nations and Nationalism*
David Graeber's *Debt: the First 5000 Years*
Antonio Gramsci's *The Prison Notebooks*
Alexander Hamilton, John Jay & James Madison's *The Federalist Papers*
Friedrich Hayek's *The Road to Serfdom*
Christopher Hill's *The World Turned Upside Down*
Thomas Hobbes's *Leviathan*
John A. Hobson's *Imperialism: A Study*
Samuel P. Huntington's *The Clash of Civilizations and the Remaking of World Order*
Tony Judt's *Postwar: A History of Europe Since 1945*
David C. Kang's *China Rising: Peace, Power and Order in East Asia*
Paul Kennedy's *The Rise and Fall of Great Powers*
Robert Keohane's *After Hegemony*
Martin Luther King Jr.'s *Why We Can't Wait*
Henry Kissinger's *World Order: Reflections on the Character of Nations and the Course of History*
John Locke's *Two Treatises of Government*
Niccolò Machiavelli's *The Prince*
Thomas Robert Malthus's *An Essay on the Principle of Population*
Mahmood Mamdani's *Citizen and Subject: Contemporary Africa And The Legacy Of Late Colonialism*
Karl Marx's *Capital*
John Stuart Mill's *On Liberty*
John Stuart Mill's *Utilitarianism*
Hans Morgenthau's *Politics Among Nations*
Thomas Paine's *Common Sense*
Thomas Paine's *Rights of Man*
Thomas Piketty's *Capital in the Twenty-First Century*
Robert D. Putman's *Bowling Alone*
John Rawls's *Theory of Justice*
Jean-Jacques Rousseau's *The Social Contract*
Theda Skocpol's *States and Social Revolutions*
Adam Smith's *The Wealth of Nations*
Sun Tzu's *The Art of War*
Henry David Thoreau's *Civil Disobedience*
Thucydides's *The History of the Peloponnesian War*
Kenneth Waltz's *Theory of International Politics*
Max Weber's *Politics as a Vocation*
Odd Arne Westad's *The Global Cold War: Third World Interventions And The Making Of Our Times*

POSTCOLONIAL STUDIES

Roland Barthes's *Mythologies*
Frantz Fanon's *Black Skin, White Masks*
Homi K. Bhabha's *The Location of Culture*
Gustavo Gutiérrez's *A Theology of Liberation*
Edward Said's *Orientalism*
Gayatri Chakravorty Spivak's *Can the Subaltern Speak?*

PSYCHOLOGY

Gordon Allport's *The Nature of Prejudice*
Alan Baddeley & Graham Hitch's *Aggression: A Social Learning Analysis*
Albert Bandura's *Aggression: A Social Learning Analysis*
Leon Festinger's *A Theory of Cognitive Dissonance*
Sigmund Freud's *The Interpretation of Dreams*
Betty Friedan's *The Feminine Mystique*
Michael R. Gottfredson & Travis Hirschi's *A General Theory of Crime*
Eric Hoffer's *The True Believer: Thoughts on the Nature of Mass Movements*
William James's *Principles of Psychology*
Elizabeth Loftus's *Eyewitness Testimony*
A. H. Maslow's *A Theory of Human Motivation*
Stanley Milgram's *Obedience to Authority*
Steven Pinker's *The Better Angels of Our Nature*
Oliver Sacks's *The Man Who Mistook His Wife For a Hat*
Richard Thaler & Cass Sunstein's *Nudge: Improving Decisions About Health, Wealth and Happiness*
Amos Tversky's *Judgment under Uncertainty: Heuristics and Biases*
Philip Zimbardo's *The Lucifer Effect*

SCIENCE

Rachel Carson's *Silent Spring*
William Cronon's *Nature's Metropolis: Chicago And The Great West*
Alfred W. Crosby's *The Columbian Exchange*
Charles Darwin's *On the Origin of Species*
Richard Dawkin's *The Selfish Gene*
Thomas Kuhn's *The Structure of Scientific Revolutions*
Geoffrey Parker's *Global Crisis: War, Climate Change and Catastrophe in the Seventeenth Century*
Mathis Wackernagel & William Rees's *Our Ecological Footprint*

SOCIOLOGY

Michelle Alexander's *The New Jim Crow: Mass Incarceration in the Age of Colorblindness*
Gordon Allport's *The Nature of Prejudice*
Albert Bandura's *Aggression: A Social Learning Analysis*
Hanna Batatu's *The Old Social Classes And The Revolutionary Movements Of Iraq*
Ha-Joon Chang's *Kicking Away the Ladder*
W. E. B. Du Bois's *The Souls of Black Folk*
Émile Durkheim's *On Suicide*
Frantz Fanon's *Black Skin, White Masks*
Frantz Fanon's *The Wretched of the Earth*
Eric Foner's *Reconstruction: America's Unfinished Revolution, 1863-1877*
Eugene Genovese's *Roll, Jordan, Roll: The World the Slaves Made*
Jack Goldstone's *Revolution and Rebellion in the Early Modern World*
Antonio Gramsci's *The Prison Notebooks*
Richard Herrnstein & Charles A Murray's *The Bell Curve: Intelligence and Class Structure in American Life*
Eric Hoffer's *The True Believer: Thoughts on the Nature of Mass Movements*
Jane Jacobs's *The Death and Life of Great American Cities*
Robert Lucas's *Why Doesn't Capital Flow from Rich to Poor Countries?*
Jay Macleod's *Ain't No Makin' It: Aspirations and Attainment in a Low Income Neighborhood*
Elaine May's *Homeward Bound: American Families in the Cold War Era*
Douglas McGregor's *The Human Side of Enterprise*
C. Wright Mills's *The Sociological Imagination*

The Macat Library By Discipline

Thomas Piketty's *Capital in the Twenty-First Century*
Robert D. Putman's *Bowling Alone*
David Riesman's *The Lonely Crowd: A Study of the Changing American Character*
Edward Said's *Orientalism*
Joan Wallach Scott's *Gender and the Politics of History*
Theda Skocpol's *States and Social Revolutions*
Max Weber's *The Protestant Ethic and the Spirit of Capitalism*

THEOLOGY

Augustine's *Confessions*
Benedict's *Rule of St Benedict*
Gustavo Gutiérrez's *A Theology of Liberation*
Carole Hillenbrand's *The Crusades: Islamic Perspectives*
David Hume's *Dialogues Concerning Natural Religion*
Immanuel Kant's *Religion within the Boundaries of Mere Reason*
Ernst Kantorowicz's *The King's Two Bodies: A Study in Medieval Political Theology*
Søren Kierkegaard's *The Sickness Unto Death*
C. S. Lewis's *The Abolition of Man*
Saba Mahmood's *The Politics of Piety: The Islamic Revival and the Feminist Subjec*t
Baruch Spinoza's *Ethics*
Keith Thomas's *Religion and the Decline of Magic*

COMING SOON

Chris Argyris's *The Individual and the Organisation*
Seyla Benhabib's *The Rights of Others*
Walter Benjamin's *The Work Of Art in the Age of Mechanical Reproduction*
John Berger's *Ways of Seeing*
Pierre Bourdieu's *Outline of a Theory of Practice*
Mary Douglas's *Purity and Danger*
Roland Dworkin's *Taking Rights Seriously*
James G. March's *Exploration and Exploitation in Organisational Learning*
Ikujiro Nonaka's *A Dynamic Theory of Organizational Knowledge Creation*
Griselda Pollock's *Vision and Difference*
Amartya Sen's *Inequality Re-Examined*
Susan Sontag's *On Photography*
Yasser Tabbaa's *The Transformation of Islamic Art*
Ludwig von Mises's *Theory of Money and Credit*

Macat Disciplines

*Access the greatest ideas and thinkers
across entire disciplines, including*

MACAT

AFRICANA STUDIES

Chinua Achebe's *An Image of Africa:
Racism in Conrad's Heart of Darkness*

W. E. B. Du Bois's *The Souls of Black Folk*

Zora Neale Hurston's *Characteristics of Negro Expression*

Martin Luther King Jr.'s *Why We Can't Wait*

Toni Morrison's *Playing in the Dark:
Whiteness in the American Literary Imagination*

Macat Disciplines

Access the greatest ideas and thinkers across entire disciplines, including

FEMINISM, GENDER AND QUEER STUDIES

Simone De Beauvoir's
The Second Sex

Michel Foucault's
History of Sexuality

Betty Friedan's
The Feminine Mystique

Saba Mahmood's
The Politics of Piety: The Islamic Revival and the Feminist Subject

Joan Wallach Scott's
Gender and the Politics of History

Mary Wollstonecraft's
A Vindication of the Rights of Woman

Virginia Woolf's
A Room of One's Own

Judith Butler's
Gender Trouble

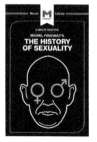

Macat Disciplines

Access the greatest ideas and thinkers across entire disciplines, including

INEQUALITY

Ha-Joon Chang's, *Kicking Away the Ladder*

David Graeber's, *Debt: The First 5000 Years*

Robert E. Lucas's, *Why Doesn't Capital Flow from Rich To Poor Countries?*

Thomas Piketty's, *Capital in the Twenty-First Century*

Amartya Sen's, *Inequality Re-Examined*

Mahbub Ul Haq's, *Reflections on Human Development*

Macat Disciplines

Access the greatest ideas and thinkers across entire disciplines, including

MACAT

CRIMINOLOGY

Michelle Alexander's
*The New Jim Crow:
Mass Incarceration in the
Age of Colorblindness*

**Michael R. Gottfredson
& Travis Hirschi's**
A General Theory of Crime

Elizabeth Loftus's
Eyewitness Testimony

**Richard Herrnstein
& Charles A. Murray's**
*The Bell Curve: Intelligence and
Class Structure in American Life*

Jay Macleod's
*Ain't No Makin' It:
Aspirations and Attainment in a
Low-Income Neighborhood*

Philip Zimbardo's
The Lucifer Effect

Macat Disciplines

Access the greatest ideas and thinkers across entire disciplines, including

Postcolonial Studies

Roland Barthes's *Mythologies*
Frantz Fanon's *Black Skin, White Masks*
Homi K. Bhabha's *The Location of Culture*
Gustavo Gutiérrez's *A Theology of Liberation*
Edward Said's *Orientalism*
Gayatri Chakravorty Spivak's *Can the Subaltern Speak?*

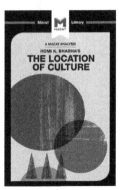

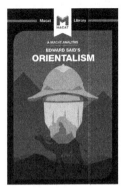

Macat Disciplines

Access the greatest ideas and thinkers across entire disciplines, including

GLOBALIZATION

Arjun Appadurai's, *Modernity at Large: Cultural Dimensions of Globalisation*

James Ferguson's, *The Anti-Politics Machine*

Geert Hofstede's, *Culture's Consequences*

Amartya Sen's, *Development as Freedom*

Macat Pairs

Analyse historical and modern issues from opposite sides of an argument. Pairs include:

HOW TO RUN AN ECONOMY

John Maynard Keynes's
The General Theory OF Employment, Interest and Money

Classical economics suggests that market economies are self-correcting in times of recession or depression, and tend toward full employment and output. But English economist John Maynard Keynes disagrees.

In his ground-breaking 1936 study *The General Theory*, Keynes argues that traditional economics has misunderstood the causes of unemployment. Employment is not determined by the price of labor; it is directly linked to demand. Keynes believes market economies are by nature unstable, and so require government intervention. Spurred on by the social catastrophe of the Great Depression of the 1930s, he sets out to revolutionize the way the world thinks

Milton Friedman's
The Role of Monetary Policy

Friedman's 1968 paper changed the course of economic theory. In just 17 pages, he demolished existing theory and outlined an effective alternate monetary policy designed to secure 'high employment, stable prices and rapid growth.'

Friedman demonstrated that monetary policy plays a vital role in broader economic stability and argued that economists got their monetary policy wrong in the 1950s and 1960s by misunderstanding the relationship between inflation and unemployment. Previous generations of economists had believed that governments could permanently decrease unemployment by permitting inflation—and vice versa. Friedman's most original contribution was to show that this supposed trade-off is an illusion that only works in the short term.

Macat analyses are available from all good bookshops and libraries.

Access hundreds of analyses through one, multimedia tool.
Join free for one month **library.macat.com**

Macat Disciplines

Access the greatest ideas and thinkers across entire disciplines, including

THE FUTURE OF DEMOCRACY

Robert A. Dahl's, *Democracy and Its Critics*
Robert A. Dahl's, *Who Governs?*
Alexis De Toqueville's, *Democracy in America*
Niccolò Machiavelli's, *The Prince*
John Stuart Mill's, *On Liberty*
Robert D. Putnam's, *Bowling Alone*
Jean-Jacques Rousseau's, *The Social Contract*
Henry David Thoreau's, *Civil Disobedience*

Macat Disciplines

Access the greatest ideas and thinkers across entire disciplines, including

TOTALITARIANISM

Sheila Fitzpatrick's, *Everyday Stalinism*
Ian Kershaw's, *The "Hitler Myth"*
Timothy Snyder's, *Bloodlands*

Macat Pairs

Analyse historical and modern issues from opposite sides of an argument. Pairs include:

RACE AND IDENTITY

Zora Neale Hurston's
Characteristics of Negro Expression

Using material collected on anthropological expeditions to the South, Zora Neale Hurston explains how expression in African American culture in the early twentieth century departs from the art of white America. At the time, African American art was often criticized for copying white culture. For Hurston, this criticism misunderstood how art works. European tradition views art as something fixed. But Hurston describes a creative process that is alive, ever-changing, and largely improvisational. She maintains that African American art works through a process called 'mimicry'—where an imitated object or verbal pattern, for example, is reshaped and altered until it becomes something new, novel—and worthy of attention.

Frantz Fanon's
Black Skin, White Masks

Black Skin, White Masks offers a radical analysis of the psychological effects of colonization on the colonized.

Fanon witnessed the effects of colonization first hand both in his birthplace, Martinique, and again later in life when he worked as a psychiatrist in another French colony, Algeria. His text is uncompromising in form and argument. He dissects the dehumanizing effects of colonialism, arguing that it destroys the native sense of identity, forcing people to adapt to an alien set of values—including a core belief that they are inferior. This results in deep psychological trauma.

Fanon's work played a pivotal role in the civil rights movements of the 1960s.

Macat analyses are available from all good bookshops and libraries.

Access hundreds of analyses through one, multimedia tool.
Join free for one month **library.macat.com**

Macat Pairs

*Analyse historical and modern issues from opposite sides of an argument.
Pairs include:*

INTERNATIONAL RELATIONS IN THE 21ST CENTURY

Samuel P. Huntington's
The Clash of Civilisations

In his highly influential 1996 book, Huntington offers a vision of a post-Cold War world in which conflict takes place not between competing ideologies but between cultures. The worst clash, he argues, will be between the Islamic world and the West: the West's arrogance and belief that its culture is a "gift" to the world will come into conflict with Islam's obstinacy and concern that its culture is under attack from a morally decadent "other."

Clash inspired much debate between different political schools of thought. But its greatest impact came in helping define American foreign policy in the wake of the 2001 terrorist attacks in New York and Washington.

Francis Fukuyama's
The End of History and the Last Man

Published in 1992, *The End of History and the Last Man* argues that capitalist democracy is the final destination for all societies. Fukuyama believed democracy triumphed during the Cold War because it lacks the "fundamental contradictions" inherent in communism and satisfies our yearning for freedom and equality. Democracy therefore marks the endpoint in the evolution of ideology, and so the "end of history." There will still be "events," but no fundamental change in ideology.

Macat Disciplines
Access the greatest ideas and thinkers across entire disciplines, including

MAN AND THE ENVIRONMENT

The Brundtland Report's, *Our Common Future*
Rachel Carson's, *Silent Spring*
James Lovelock's, *Gaia: A New Look at Life on Earth*
Mathis Wackernagel & William Rees's, *Our Ecological Footprint*

Macat Pairs

Analyse historical and modern issues from opposite sides of an argument. Pairs include:

ARE WE FUNDAMENTALLY GOOD - OR BAD?

Steven Pinker's
The Better Angels of Our Nature

Stephen Pinker's gloriously optimistic 2011 book argues that, despite humanity's biological tendency toward violence, we are, in fact, less violent today than ever before. To prove his case, Pinker lays out pages of detailed statistical evidence. For him, much of the credit for the decline goes to the eighteenth-century Enlightenment movement, whose ideas of liberty, tolerance, and respect for the value of human life filtered down through society and affected how people thought. That psychological change led to behavioral change—and overall we became more peaceful. Critics countered that humanity could never overcome the biological urge toward violence; others argued that Pinker's statistics were flawed.

Philip Zimbardo's
The Lucifer Effect

Some psychologists believe those who commit cruelty are innately evil. Zimbardo disagrees. In *The Lucifer Effect*, he argues that sometimes good people do evil things simply because of the situations they find themselves in, citing many historical examples to illustrate his point. Zimbardo details his 1971 Stanford prison experiment, where ordinary volunteers playing guards in a mock prison rapidly became abusive. But he also describes the tortures committed by US army personnel in Iraq's Abu Ghraib prison in 2003—and how he himself testified in defence of one of those guards. committed by US army personnel in Iraq's Abu Ghraib prison in 2003—and how he himself testified in defence of one of those guards.

Macat Pairs

Analyse historical and modern issues from opposite sides of an argument. Pairs include:

HOW WE RELATE TO EACH OTHER AND SOCIETY

Jean-Jacques Rousseau's
The Social Contract

Rousseau's famous work sets out the radical concept of the 'social contract': a give-and-take relationship between individual freedom and social order.

If people are free to do as they like, governed only by their own sense of justice, they are also vulnerable to chaos and violence. To avoid this, Rousseau proposes, they should agree to give up some freedom to benefit from the protection of social and political organization. But this deal is only just if societies are led by the collective needs and desires of the people, and able to control the private interests of individuals. For Rousseau, the only legitimate form of government is rule by the people.

Robert D. Putnam's
Bowling Alone

In *Bowling Alone*, Robert Putnam argues that Americans have become disconnected from one another and from the institutions of their common life, and investigates the consequences of this change.

Looking at a range of indicators, from membership in formal organizations to the number of invitations being extended to informal dinner parties, Putnam demonstrates that Americans are interacting less and creating less "social capital" – with potentially disastrous implications for their society.

It would be difficult to overstate the impact of *Bowling Alone*, one of the most frequently cited social science publications of the last half-century.

Printed in the United States
by Baker & Taylor Publisher Services